D0872378

Incident at Bitter Creek

Incident at Bitter Creek

THE STORY OF THE ROCK SPRINGS
CHINESE MASSACRE

Craig Storti

Iowa State University Press / Ames

Craig Storti, Washington, D.C., is a writer, teacher, partner in the Business Communications Group, and founder of an intercultural training business.

© 1991 Iowa State University Press, Ames, Iowa 50010

Manufactured in the United States of America
⊛ This book is printed on acid-free paper.

First edition, 1991

Library of Congress Cataloging-in-Publication Data

Storti, Craig.
    Incident at Bitter Creek : the story of the Rock Springs Chinese massacre / Craig Storti. — 1st ed.
        p.   cm.
    Includes bibliographical references.
    Includes index.
    ISBN 0–8138–1403–0 (alk. paper)
    1. Chinese Americans—Wyoming—Rock Springs—History—19th century. 2. Massacres—Wyoming—Rock Springs—History—19th century. 3. Rock Springs (Wyo.)—Race relations. I. Title.
    F769.R6S76 1991
    978.7'85—dc20   90–43478

For my mother

with love and gratitude

CONTENTS

ACKNOWLEDGMENTS

I AM GRATEFUL TO A NUMBER OF INDIVIDUALS who helped me in the making of this book. To begin with, I would like to express my gratitude to my brother, Bob Storti, and his wife, Nora, for picking me up at airports, housing and feeding me, lending me various cars, and generally taking such good care of me during several research trips to Wyoming.

And while we are still in Sweetwater County, I would also like to thank the friendly, kind, and patient—not to mention knowledgeable—people at the County Historical Museum in Green River. They answered scores of foolish questions, inspired the odd intelligent one, and rendered a variety of other services too numerous to mention. My sincere thanks, then, to Henry Chadey, May Wright, Ruth Lauritzen, and Lois Brandner.

Further afield, I would like to thank Jean Brainerd at the State Archives in Cheyenne, Don Snoddy, formerly with the Nebraska State Historical Society in Lincoln, and Emmet Chisum at the University of Wyoming library. These kind souls led me ever deeper into primary sources and patiently responded to virtually all of my whims.

For their tireless support and encouragement, which included—but by no means was limited to—their shrewd comments on my first draft, I am very grateful to Joseph Coyle and Sally Di Paula.

I would like to single out Tanya Zelenkov for special mention: when I finished my first draft, I knew there was a book hiding in there somewhere—and Tanya found it for me. I will always be grateful.

Finally, I want to thank my wife Charlotte for calmly leading me past the inevitable crises of confidence. And for so much more. It's an open question whether it's harder to write a book or to live with someone who's writing a book, but I suspect the latter may be the greater achievement.

INTRODUCTION

Give me your tired, your poor,
Your huddled masses yearning to breathe free,
The wretched refuse of your teeming shore,
Send these tempest-tost to me,
I lift my lamp beside the golden door!
                                    —EMMA LAZARUS

L ess than two years after the poet Emma Lazarus wrote those
words for the base of the Statue of Liberty, they were no longer
true. In 1888, in the midst of a hotly contested presidential
election campaign, Congress passed the Exclusion Act, effectively
barring any future Chinese immigration to the United States. "The
golden door," so far as the sojourner from the Celestial Kingdom was
concerned, had suddenly slammed shut.

Incident at Bitter Creek is a retelling of one of the pivotal and most
dramatic episodes in the unraveling of a fundamental American ideal:
free and open immigration. As such, it is a story about the loss of
innocence and the coming of age of a young nation just entering its
second century. It is also a story about the consequences of the failure
of the Chinese to become integrated into American culture—about
what happened to a race of people who did not blend into the
American melting pot.

But it is something else besides. While it has been called "one of
the bloodiest race riots in the nation's history,"[1] the Rock Springs
Chinese massacre was more than a clash between two races; it was one
of the more tragic incidents in a larger struggle between labor and
monopoly capitalism for control of the American workplace. The
much-despised Chinese sojourner, the spoiler who broke strikes and
underbid the American laborer at every turn, was a catalyst in this
wider war—and his fate was decided therein—but in the end the
killing in Rock Springs, the Exclusion Act, and the whole tumultuous
history of the Chinese in America had little to do with race prejudice

or immigration policy. The issue, rather, was the status of the American workingman in the industrial era.

Years ago, a student of the Rock Springs massacre predicted that one day there would be a book about the incident. It would be written, he said, "when some sensational story writer smells the blood and [decides] that gore sells."[2] There *was* blood that afternoon in Rock Springs, but the drama of the incident at Bitter Creek lies elsewhere, in the story of the lowly Wyoming coal miner who took on the mighty Union Pacific Railway Company in a desperate and ultimately tragic struggle for self-respect and survival.

Incident at Bitter Creek

Guests of the Golden Mountain

They have regarded California as a land of abundance . . .
and have flown thither as the wild geese fly.
                                        —LI HUNG TSAO

In early February of 1848, Chun Ming wrote a letter to his friend Chang Yum in Canton. Chun, one of approximately ten Chinese in the United States at the time, was living in San Francisco, a collection of adobe huts beside the bay. He happened to be present one afternoon when a Mormon elder named Brennan rode in out of the hills with the startling news that gold had just been discovered at a place called Coloma, thirty-five miles northeast of Sacramento. Chun joined the dash to Coloma and before long was writing his friend in Canton about gold nuggets as big as peas. Chang Yum told others. In 1849, three hundred Chinese sailed for America; in 1851, twenty-seven hundred; in 1852, twenty thousand.

The gold rush came at a crucial moment in the history of the Celestial Kingdom. Nearly all the immigrants who came to America were from the province of Canton on the southeast coast, and over 60 percent from the district of Toishan alone. Conditions in the Pearl River delta at midcentury were grim even for China, used as it was to natural and man-made disasters on a scale hard to imagine outside of Asia. Toishan a large rocky plateau standing some one thousand feet above the sea, was becoming dangerously overcrowded. The great Taiping Rebellion was in full swing, a catastrophic fourteen-year struggle against the ruling Manchu dynasty, which devastated and impoverished south China and left an astonishing thirty million

3

people dead. The landless and homeless peasants who survived descended in waves on the coastal provinces in search of a livelihood. In Toishan, the size of the average family landholding dropped from two acres to less than half an acre, barely enough to sustain a family for four months. In 1849, a terrible flood struck Canton, killing ten thousand people and leaving thousands more homeless. "The rains have been falling for 40 days," noted a memorial to the emperor, "until the rivers and the seas and the lakes and the streams have joined in one sheet over the land . . . and there is no outlet by which the waters may retire."[1] News of the discovery of the "Mountain of Gold" in California seemed too good to be true.

Even then, for a Chinese to emigrate to America—for a Chinese to emigrate anywhere—went against the very fiber of his being. Theirs was, after all, the Celestial Kingdom, the Middle Kingdom, halfway between earth and paradise, the ultimate expression of the perfectibility of man, a model of social, artistic, and political sophistication unrivaled anywhere in the world. Emigrate to where? For what? The paint on the model may have been chipped and peeling by 1850, especially in the wake of the Taiping Rebellion, but there were numerous other reasons for a man—and nearly all the immigrants were male—not to leave China. The social system was founded on the principle of subordination: the individual to the group, the young to the aged, and, especially, the living to their ancestors. Even if a man's father or grandfather gave him permission to leave, which wasn't likely, the spirits of one's ancestors would never consent, for the happiness of the souls of the departed, it was believed, depended on yearly visits by family members to the gravesite, visits that must be made in person and not by some priestly proxy. And nothing troubled a Chinese more than the wrath of an ancestral spirit.

There were other reasons. Unlike the great majority of the Irish and other European immigrants to America at this time, over half the Chinese who came were married, leaving behind not only their country but, for a period at least, a wife and family. There was also the fact that under the Manchu regime, emigration was against the law. "Any official responsible for the arrest of ten illegal immigrants," one decree declared, "shall be accorded one merit toward his promotion; if of one-hundred such culprits, his reward shall be promotion to the next higher rank."[2] The punishment for emigration was beheading.

And still they went. Letters told of instant fortune. At Moore's Flat two Chinese found a 240-pound gold nugget worth $30,000. For those not so lucky, there were jobs that paid astonishing wages. In

China the average wage in 1850 was $3 to $5 a month; in California it was $1 a day. In two months a man could make what it would take him a year to earn in China. In three years he could earn enough to last him a lifetime. Such opportunity in the face of such a terrible need—perhaps the spirits of one's ancestors would understand. Or so the Gum Shan Hok, as they were called, the Guests of the Golden Mountain, told themselves.

In the early years nearly all the Chinese who came were men, 70 percent between the ages of twenty and thirty-nine, and they all came with the same purpose: to make a "pile." With that pile they would then return to China and buy themselves and their families out of the bonds of tenant farming, the clutches of moneylenders, or the servitude of feudalism. Often the family raised the money for the sojourner's passage or, if they were too poor, put up their house or their land or a brother's labor as collateral for money lent by someone else. Then the sojourner—the traveler who will one day return—paid off the loan from his earnings in America.

That was how an emigrant chose to go if he could, but many families had neither money nor collateral, and the would-be sojourner had to buy his passage with the promise of his labor. In Hong Kong or Canton he contacted the recruiting agent of a rich Chinese businessman in America, who in turn was usually the labor contractor for an American entrepreneur, and agreed to work for a specified period in exchange for passage. The well-informed emigrant shunned this scheme, for he knew that at $30 a month, an average wage, he could pay back the $50 passage fee in three or four months, whereas the contracted laborer was obliged to work for a minimum of six months, and more often a year, before he was released. But there was no shortage of applicants. They called themselves "koo lee" (coolie, or "hired muscle"), and they came by the thousands.

But many a coolie bought his name less willingly. Just in from the country, passage money in his pocket, he was befriended by an "agent," treated to dinner and all he could drink, and taken for a turn at the gambling tables. The next morning, his pockets empty, too ashamed to go back and face his family, he signed where the agent indicated and became a coolie. He was free to refuse (but few did), and even then he might be kidnapped, or "shanghaied" as it was known, and shipped off anyway.

He leaves from his village, our uncertain emigrant, carrying a bedroll and a bamboo basket. In the basket he has his hat, shoes, and provisions for the journey. At the river he bids farewell to his family and hires a junk or sampan for the first leg of his trip. Many sampans later, he arrives in Hong Kong. He makes his way to the waterfront, is recruited, and puts up in a dormitory until his ship is scheduled to leave. He has never been more than a mile or two from his home, and now, on the morrow, he leaves on a journey that will take him a third of the way around the world.

Seven thousand miles, two months across the Pacific to the shores of the Golden Mountain. The route leads up the China coast to the Formosa strait, around the northern end of the island to avoid the trade winds, and then east from Japan between 35 and 45 degrees latitude in the path of the westerlies. Until 1867, all the boats are clipper ships, of the cargo persuasion: passengers below deck, merchandise on top. The sojourner stays in the cramped, stuffy hold, sleeping on a narrow bunk, cooking over an open brazier. He can hardly see for the smoke or breathe in the airless confinement. To pass the time, he gambles and walks about the deck. On calm days, when there is no wind to lift the sails, tempers flare.

At the pier in San Francisco, all is chaos; agents pushing and shoving to round up their coolies, other agents fighting one another to hire sojourners who have come on their own, still others shouting out the room-and-board rates of cheap hotels or the price of cut-rate tickets to the goldfields. There is a crush of baskets, bedrolls, wide-brimmed hats, and bamboo poles. A crowd has gathered, just to watch. At last the new arrivals are sorted out and marched single file through the streets to company dormitories and a meal of fried rice, bamboo shoots, and mushrooms, all washed down with native tea and weak rice wine. The next morning or the day after, he takes a steamer upriver to the gold country, and his sojourn in America begins.

While most of the Chinese who came in the 1850s worked in mining, almost none were the fortune-hunting prospectors of myth and movies. (Few whites were either.) They were, rather, wage earners working claims owned by the companies whose agents had hired them. They were paid a daily salary for their services, and any gold they took out belonged to the company, which often as not was owned by wealthy businessmen in San Francisco, New York, or London. A few Chinese pooled their resources with others from their home district and struck out on their own, but for the most part the attraction of the Golden Mountain was simply the $30 a month the sojourner could earn while making other men fabulously rich. Most of the claims the sojourners worked, for others or for themselves, were "dead," played out and abandoned by previous prospectors and bought up by the gold companies. The gold in these claims lay embedded in quartz and was profitable only when mined on a large scale with cheap labor.

Chinese who did not work in the goldfields found service jobs in the many mining camps springing up throughout the Sierra Nevada. Still others did domestic work in San Francisco. During the boom years of the gold rush, there was no one to cook or wash clothes. The men of San Francisco, rubes and dandies alike, thought nothing of sending their dirty shirts to Honolulu or Hong Kong and waiting four months to get them back. The Chinese quietly filled the gap, opening restaurants and laundries throughout the city and in other cities. In the camps, a miner paid $12 to have a dozen pieces of laundry washed; in San Francisco, the Chinese did it for $6. For every ten dozen shirts he washed, the sojourner made $60, a year's wage in the Celestial Kingdom.

Slowly, throughout the 1850s, their numbers grew. In the first three months of 1849, no ship brought more than 10 sojourners. On October 15, the *Amazon* brought 101. A month later, at the first official meeting of Chinese residents in America, 300 Chinese gathered at the Canton restaurant in San Francisco. During the first six months of 1852, eighty-two ships made the trip from Hong Kong. On March 26th that same year, 604 sojourners arrived; on a single day in 1854, 840. By the end of the decade, there were 42,000, one-quarter of the foreign-born population of California.

As early as 1852, the return was already in full swing. That year the *Wild Pigeon* became one of the first ships to take back more Chinese than it delivered. Yet the return only fanned the flames, and net immigration increased every year: "These singular men came to San Francisco a year or two ago, with a few packages of tea or rice, and by their frugality, industry, and strict attention to business, have all made money and some of them amassed fortunes. [Upon their arrival] in the Celestial Empire they will doubtless give a very favorable impression of the golden land and many more of their countrymen will come here to try their fortunes."[3]

The sojourner's industry and frugality became legendary. "Here's John Chinaman," went a popular jingle, "sitting on a fence / Trying to make a dollar / out of fifteen cents." But in fact many Chinese came by these qualities as a birthright, for industry and frugality were all but essential to survival in a place like Toishan and were not, as a rule, a sign of distinction. Only in America, where living conditions were so much more favorable and opportunity rampant, were the sojourner's innate frugality and industry by themselves the foundation of a fortune. This was the real "gold" whereof the Golden Mountain sparkled.

In the beginning, when times were good, the sojourner was welcomed with outstretched arms. "One of the most worthy of our newly-adopted citizens," Governor MacDougal called them.[4] The mayor of San Francisco invited them to participate in the funeral services for President Taylor in August 1850, and the "China boys," decked out in their finest native costumes, stole the show. And they stole it again in 1852 on the occasion of Washington's birthday. "The China boys," gushed the *Daily Alta* (California), "will yet vote at the same polls, study at the same schools and bow at the same altar as our own countrymen."[5] And "it may not be many years," the paper noted on another occasion, "before the halls of Congress are graced by the presence of a long-queued Mandarin sitting, voting, and speaking beside a *don* from Santa Fe and a Kanaker from Hawaii."[6]

The editor of another paper, the *Pacific News*, traced the sojourners' appeal to "their industry, their quietness, cheerfulness and the cleanliness of their personal habits. Whatever the white man scourned to do the Chinaman took up; whatever white men did the Chinaman could do; he was a gap-filler ... adapting himself to the white man's tastes, and slipping away, unprotestingly, to other tasks when the white man wanted his job."[7]

The brief honeymoon reached its peak at ceremonies marking California's admission to the Union in 1852. It was a great day for the new state and its colorful array of new citizens, the Chinese the most colorful of all. "Born and reared under different Governments," Justice Bennett rhapsodized as he welcomed the Chinese delegation, "and speaking different tongues, we nevertheless meet here today as brothers. ... You stand among us in all respects as equals. Henceforth we have one country, one hope, one destiny."[8]

It is known as "the period of favor," these early years of Chinese immigration when the sojourner went quietly about his business and then slipped away when he had accomplished his purpose. But in time, the sojourner became too visible on the Pacific slope; there were too many of him, especially after the completion of the transcontinental railroad, for which more than ten thousand Chinese were brought over. He could no longer go about his business quietly. Indeed, more often than not, *his* business was now the same as the white man's. And for this he could not be forgiven.

1

The Chinese Must Go

During their entire settlement in California they have never adapted themselves to our habits [or] mode of dress, never discovered the difference between right and wrong, never ceased the worship of their idol gods. They remain the same stolid Asiatics that have floated on the rivers and slaved in the fields of China for thirty centuries.

—CALIFORNIA SENATE ADDRESS
AND MEMORIAL

T he saga of the Chinese in America took a dramatic turn on July 1, 1862, when Congress passed "an act to aid in the construction of a railroad and telegraph line from the Missouri River to the Pacific." Two great companies stepped forward to undertake the massive enterprise: the Union Pacific (UP), to build west from Omaha, and the Central Pacific (CP), building east from Sacramento. For their efforts each company was paid a subsidy for every mile of track completed and, more importantly, granted a section of the land bordering each completed mile. This arrangement was necessary if investors were to have any hope of recouping their capital. At the same time, by turning the grand undertaking into a race—a spirited competition for these invaluable land grants—it lent the whole affair an air of tension and high drama.

At the height of construction, in 1868, nearly twenty-five thousand men and fifteen thousand mules and horses took to the field, the greatest concentration of labor, capital, and materials the country had ever seen in peacetime. In time the new railroad broke every record on the books: the highest railroad elevation in America (8,242 feet, the summit of the Black Hills), the highest railroad bridge in the world (127 feet, over Dale Creek near Laramie), the highest cost per mile of track ($100,000), and the most track ever laid in a single day (10 miles). Even today, the construction of the transcontinental railroad (as it was known) is still regarded as the greatest engineering feat of the nineteenth century.

It is one of the great quintessentially American tales: a stirring demonstration of what the young country, then approaching its centennial, was all about; how money, muscle, and industrial might—plus Yankee ingenuity and a dash of arrogance—could overcome any obstacle, tame any landscape, and bend the forces of nature to their will. It was America at its best.

Never mind that half of the great railroad, and the hardest half at that, was built by the Chinese.

Ah Ling was Charlie Crocker's manservant. Crocker, the chief construction engineer for the CP, had a serious labor problem. He'd advertised for workers up and down the coast and in all the mining camps. He needed five thousand men; six hundred were interested. But they no sooner arrived at end-of-track in the Sierra Nevada than they stole away to the silver fields in Carson City or to the gold mines just discovered in Montana. "These men are as near to brutes as they can get," Charlie complained, and he began negotiations with the Union army to ship five thousand Confederate prisoners from the battlefields of the East.[1] Then the war ended. He hired every Indian he could find, but he couldn't find very many.

Charlie told his assistant they ought to try the Chinese. "I will not boss Chinese," Jim Strobridge replied. "I don't think they could build a railroad."[2] Leland Stanford, president of the CP and one of Crocker's partners, was also reluctant; he had rather loudly and publicly advocated the exclusion of the Chinese from California and was loath to reverse himself. A local California newspaper got wind of the idea "to build a railroad over the Sierras with rice-eating weaklings" and promptly pronounced it "rank nonsense."[3]

But Crocker had seen Ah Ling at work and thought he knew better. As the year 1865 opened, the few workers the company had were threatening to strike. With the government paying from $14,000 to $48,000 for every mile of track laid and throwing in those generous land grants besides, the CP, if it wanted to stay solvent, would have to have more labor at once. That February, Charlie ordered fifty sojourners put on a train in Sacramento and shipped to end-of-track:

> They disembarked, glanced without curiosity at the surrounding forest, then tranquilly established camp, cooked a meal of rice and dried cuttle fish and went to sleep. By sunrise they were at work with

picks, shovels, and wheelbarrows. At the end of their first twelve hours of plodding industry, Crocker and his engineers viewed the results with gratified astonishment. Those who through the day had been momentarily expecting the weaklings to fall in their tracks from exhaustion permanently revised their opinion of the Chinaman's endurance.[4]

Crocker brought them in by the trainload, 3,000 by fall, and sent agents to China for more. He told Strobridge to put them on masonry as well. "Make masons out of Chinamen?" Strobridge asked. "Sure," Crocker answered. "Didn't they build the Great Wall?"[5] And so they became masons too. By winter there were 7,000. At the peak of construction, in 1868, over 12,000 sojourners were at work on the CP, more than a quarter of all the Chinese in America.

If they could do the work, Charlie had his men, but crossing the Sierra Nevada would not be easy. The sheer granite cliffs and gorges of the great range rose 7,000 feet in 100 miles, 2,000 feet in one 20-mile stretch alone. The UP, by comparison, building across the High Plains, rose only 5,000 feet in 500 miles, with 50 miles to climb the 2,000 feet to the top of the Black Hills— "baby work," one writer called it, next to the challenge of the Sierra Nevada.

Supplies were another problem. Every rail and spike; every crowbar, fishplate, pick, and shovel; every keg of blasting powder; even the locomotives and cars—everything had to be bought in the East and shipped fifteen thousand miles around the Horn to California. The trip could take as long as 112 days. At any one time, as many as thirty ships were on the seas to guarantee an uninterrupted flow of materials and construction. The expense was enormous, roughly four times what the UP was paying.

Crocker sent wave after wave of sojourners against the Sierra Nevada. Graders felled trees, exploded stumps, built mile after mile of earthworks, and filled in countless ravines and gullies. Where the line cut through rock, pick-and-shovel crews chiseled away at the granite, collecting the rubble in wagons and wheeling it to the brink of the nearest precipice. When the cut was too narrow for wagons, the Chinese formed basket brigades and handed the debris from man to man out to the dumping ground. They did the blasting too, threading their way along narrow paths with seventy-pound kegs of gunpowder dangling from either end of bamboo poles slung over their shoulders. They drilled the holes, placed the charges, cut and set the fuses, and ran for cover.

Cape Horn was their finest hour. This sheer granite cliff soaring two thousand feet over the gorge cut by the American River was too steep and smooth for footholds. The Chinese were suspended in rope-held baskets over the face of the great wall as they chipped and chiseled a narrow ledge out of the rock, swaying all the while in the fierce winds that blew through the canyon. When the ledge was wide enough, other Chinese crept out on all fours and deepened it into a shelf broad enough to receive tracks. The whole business took a full year, but when it was finished, there was no longer any doubt about the capacities of the sojourner.

Strobridge led the chorus of praise: "They learn all parts of the job easily," he remarked, and later called them "the best roadbuilders in the world."[6] Crocker was happy on all counts: "If we were in a hurry," he told a congressional committee, "it was better to put Chinese on at once. They could cut more rock in a week than the Cornish miners. . . . They were trustworthy, intelligent, and they lived up to their contracts."[7]

Even company president Stanford, no longer preaching exclusion, was won over: "Without the Chinese," he wrote President Andrew Johnson, "it would be impossible to complete the western portion of this great national enterprise."[8] (Stanford later included in his will a provision for the permanent employment of a large number of Chinese on his estates.) "Crocker's pets," as they were called, were here to stay.

The Chinese made up 80 percent of the Central Pacific's work force, filling all positions except foreman and tracklayer, which were held by the Irish. They worked in gangs of fifteen to twenty men, each gang with its own headman and cook. They lived in boxcars, tents, or plank shacks and ate on the ground with chopsticks. They usually wore their native dress—blue cotton smocks and trousers and "basket" hats—but many bought American shoes, which were invariably too big. They worked six days a week, dawn to dusk, and were paid $28 a month, of which they saved nearly two-thirds. Relations with the whites around them were cordial, correct, and for the most part nonexistent.

The exception was Charlie Crocker. He loved his pets and they loved their "Cholly." Crocker had come to California in the gold rush but soon discovered that outfitting prospectors was more profitable than being one and accordingly opened a merchandise store in San Francisco. He prospered and eventually became one of the "Big Four"—Crocker (engineer), Stanford (president), C. P. Huntington (vice president), and Mark Hopkins (treasurer)—who took on the job

Charlie Crocker.

of building the CP. A big burly Irishman (Crocker weighed 250 pounds, whereas the average Chinaman weighed 100), "raging like a mad bull in the railway camps,"[9] Crocker tramped up and down the line on his sorrel mare, urging on Irish and Chinese alike in the great race against the UP. He loved nothing more than to ride into camp on payday in his bearskin overcoat, his beard tinged with snow, his horse steaming, saddlebags bulging, and call out the names of sojourners and "Paddies" and drop the gold and silver coins into their outstretched hands. If anyone could lay a trail of iron over the Sierra Nevada, for years an open question, Charlie Crocker was the man.

But he was sorely tested. The winter of 1865–1866 was one of the worst on record in the mountains. Snow began falling in October, and one storm followed another for the next five months. The tracks lay buried under an average of fifteen feet of snow, with drifts up to sixty. Five locomotives failed to push a snowplow through, and Charlie had to assign forty-five hundred men, half his work force, just to keep the tracks, hence the supply lines, open.

Tunnels were dug beneath forty-foot drifts and for months three-thousand workmen lived curious, mole-like lives, passing from work to living quarters in dim passages far beneath the snow's surface. This eerie existence was complicated by constant danger, for as snows accumulated on the upper ridges, avalanches grew frequent, their approach heralded only by a thunderous roar. A second later, a work crew, a bunkhouse, sometimes an entire camp, would go hurtling at a dizzy speed down miles of frozen canyons. Not until months later were the bodies recovered; sometimes groups were found with shovels or picks still clutched in their frozen hands.[10]

Stymied by the weather, Charlie unleashed his army on the summit tunnels, ten in number, that had to be cut through solid rock along a twenty-five-mile stretch of the road between Cisco and Lake Ridge. Nine thousand Chinese led the assault, working day and night in three eight-hour shifts. The rock was so hard, it dented and flattened their picks and shovels. Gunpowder was then brought in, five hundred kegs a day, and still the rock would not yield. Out in Nebraska, the UP laid a mile of track a day; here at the summit of the Rockies, the Chinese, on a good day, managed twenty-seven inches.

Desperate, Crocker brought in a Swedish chemist named Swanson who had recently perfected the technique of mixing glycerine with nitric and sulfuric acid to make a powerful explosive. The mixture was so volatile that a single drop, spilled by a man as he walked, would explode and destroy him without leaving a trace. The Chinese refused to touch it. They drilled holes for this nitroglycerine and cut and set the fuses, but they let white men carry it and pour it into the rock. After the explosion, the Chinese returned to clear away the rubble. On several occasions, whole crews of Chinese were blown to pieces when their picks struck hidden pockets of the unexploded liquid. Crocker limited use of the dangerous compound to especially difficult tunnels and finally gave up using it altogether. Small wonder the phrase "not a Chinaman's chance" was born that winter and spring in the Sierra Nevada. In all, the building of the CP cost the lives of over twelve hundred Chinese, one out of every ten Charlie Crocker signed up.

The tunnels' combined length was 1,695 feet, and they took thirteen months to complete. Track cost per mile for the CP in 1866 was $280,000; the most expensive mile the UP laid cost only $80,000. Total track laid in 1866: 20 miles for the CP, 265 for its rival.

Incredibly, the winter of 1866–1867 was even worse than the one before. Forty-four storms lashed the Sierra. In the worst, snow began falling at 2:00 P.M. on February 18 and fell without pause until 10:00 P.M. four days later. Five thousand Chinese shoveled snow to keep the line open. Crocker suspended all grading in the mountains and sent three thousand more Chinese three hundred miles ahead to begin grading in Palisade Canyon. Then, to keep them supplied, he had trees cut and laid side by side on the snow to make a "road" for locomotives and cars that were pulled along on log sleds greased with lard. Once over the mountains, the supplies were transferred to wagons and hauled across the desert to the canyon by mules. The scheme cost triple what it would to do the same job in the summer, but by working through the winter—that one and the one before—Crocker shortened construction time by seven years from what Congress expected.

By August 1867, the Chinese completed bore work on the tunnels, and by November, rails were laid over the summit and on down the eastern slopes. On December 13, end-of-track pushed past State Line into Nevada. After three years, the Rockies had been tamed. Total track for 1867: 47 miles for Crocker and company, 247 for the UP.

After the Rockies, the Nevada desert was child's play; no gullies to fill in, no rock to cut through, just turn and tamp the earth, and keep an eye out for lizards and tarantulas. This was classic railroad building of the sort the UP had been doing all along. But now the contest was even, and Charlie and his Celestials threw themselves into the race with great gusto. When Jack Casement, Crocker's counterpart on the UP, wired that his men had laid an extraordinary six miles of track in one day, a record in the history of railroad construction, Crocker's men turned around and laid seven. "No damn Chinks shall beat my boys at track laying," Casement swore, and he promptly told select track gangs to take a three-day rest. On the fourth day, working into the night by the light of lanterns, Casement's men laid seven and one-half miles of iron road. Crocker wired "to whomever it may concern" that he would lay ten. Casement bet him $10,000 that he couldn't. Crocker waited for the right moment.

Visitors to the scene, mostly journalists and dignitaries from the East, were astonished at the spectacle and the pace of construction. With four years of experience behind them, both companies had railroad building down to a science.

Supplies from Omaha or Sacramento are piled onto cars—a single mile of track requires the contents of forty cars—and brought over the road to end-of-track. When the supplies arrive, men slip away the slats holding the materials in place. Rails, ties, kegs of spikes spill to the ground. Ties are thrown into wagons, whisked to end-of-track, laid out side by side on the finely graded roadbed. Back-iron men load rails onto a horse-drawn lorry. The lorry mounts the tracks in front of the engine, pulls the rails to waiting front-iron men. From either side two men seize the front of a rail and pull it off over the roller on the front

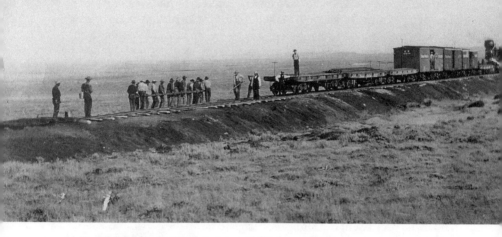

Tracklayers on the intercontinental. (Photograph from The Sweetwater County Historical Museum, Green River, Wyoming)

of the lorry while two others grab the back end as it slips free. The four men run forward, drop the rail, return for another. Four others do the same with the parallel rail. Thirty seconds per rail, 4 rails a minute, 440 rails per mile, four miles a day. Each rail weighs four hundred pounds. Each man lifts two hundred pounds every minute, six tons every hour, fifty tons every day.

Spike peddlers toss two spikes per crosstie along each rail. Gaugers step up and align the new rail to the one behind. Head-spikers step up, fit ten spikes to the holes in each rail, strike each spike once. Back-spikers follow, 2 blows per spike; 30 blows per rail, 12,660 blows per mile, fifteen hundred miles Omaha to Sacramento.

Screwers step forward, mount fishplates where two rails meet. Back-fillers shovel dirt between ties, tamp it down to prop up the road. Track-liners step up, wielding crowbars to jack the line straight. When the rail lorry is empty, teamsters yank it from the track to make way for the one already waiting just behind. Now the iron men step forward again, seize a rail, pull it off over the roller. Water carriers are everywhere. The Chinese do every job except for rail-handling.

The whole operation was like a giant factory, complete with its factory town, inching its way across America, a factory whose daily output was two or three miles of laid railroad track. It was simply the application of the principles of mass production and specialization of labor to a location that happened to be moving.

Journalists could scarcely contain their enthusiasm. "We pundits of the East," wrote a reporter for the Philadelphia *Bulletin*,

> stood upon that embankment . . . and backed westward before that hurrying corps of sturdy operatives with a mingled feeling of amusement, curiosity and profound respect.
>
> Sherman with his victorious legions, sweeping from Atlanta to Savannah, was a spectacle less glorious than this army of men, marching on foot from Omaha to Sacramento, subduing unknown wilderness, scaling unknown mountains, surmounting untried obstacles, and binding across the broad breast of America the iron emblem of modern progress and civilization. All honor to the indomitable wills, the brave hearts, and the brawny muscles that are actually achieving the great work.[11]

Building the railroad across the High Plains. (Photograph from The Sweetwater County Historical Museum, Green River, Wyoming)

The CP made good time across Nevada. With the road behind them open all the way to the coast, rails arrived as fast as track gangs could lay them, four miles a day by mid-March. Crocker even worked his crews at night, by the light of great sagebrush bonfires. The only problems were Paiutes and the lack of water. The company spent thousands of dollars drilling wells and thousands more on water trains and tank wagons, hauling water up to forty miles from the nearest source to the graders out in front of the construction. In the desert beyond the Truckee and Humboldt rivers, it was so dry that "even jack-rabbits carried a canteen and a haversack."[12]

The Paiutes frightened the Chinese, by their presence and by the stories they told of giant snakes out in the desert, big enough to swallow a man whole. The sojourners asked Charlie for protection. The wily Crocker met with the chiefs and promised them and their braves free railroad passes in exchange for safe passage for the construction crews; the braves would have to ride in freight cars, Crocker noted, but the chiefs could ride first-class.

In late November, the CP reached Palisade Canyon, all graded and waiting, and Charlie established end-of-track at Elko, 464 miles from Sacramento. Mileage for the year was 362 (vs. 425 for the UP), three times the total of all track laid by the CP since the beginning of construction.

Less than three hundred miles separated the two lines now, and in the spring of 1869, rival grading crews, working fifty to seventy-five miles ahead of track gangs, met and passed each other, laying down parallel roadbeds across more than one hundred miles of Utah. At night they stole each other's fill. One night the Paddies of the UP set a charge that exploded on the Chinese. The next night the Chinese retaliated.* Finally, on April 9, Congress declared the two lines would meet at Promontory Point, north of Salt Lake City. The race was over.

There remained the matter of Crocker's boast: ten miles in a single day. He waited until only sixteen miles separated the two lines and then assembled a crew of eight of his best rail-handlers. On the morning of April 28, five thousand spectators gathered in the crisp

---

*One wag wrote a poem about it:
> Last week a premature blast went off,
> And a mile in the sky went big Jim Guff.
> Now when next payday came round,
> Jim Guff a dollar short was found.
> He asked the reason; came the reply,
> "You were docked for the time you were up in the sky."

Utah dawn to witness the reckoning: "The Central Pacific had its grade made and its ties in place on the morning of the test, and cars loaded with rails stood ready for the starting signal, and men with nippers, four men to each rail, stood ready to carry the rails from the cars to the ties. Another crew was ready with fastenings and spikes, the crew of drivers was ready, and lastly, a crew of shovelers was ready to surface the newly laid track."[13]

The eight rail-handlers were Irish; the other crews were all Chinese.

At seven sharp, the first lorry-load of iron pulled up, and the countdown began. The terrain was straight and level; in the first eight seconds, 240 feet were laid. The lorry moved steadily forward, its horses changed every two hours. By 1:30 P.M., six miles were down, and the track gang broke for a leisurely lunch (and all five thousand spectators dined on the CP). At 2:30, they were back at work, the terrain steeper and winding now. They lost an hour bending rails. Crocker offered to call in a reserve gang, but the original eight wouldn't hear of it. The crowd shuffled along, shouting encouragement. At the stroke of 7:00, they were whistled to a halt. Ten miles and 1,800 feet to spare. The eight Irishmen had handled nearly a million pounds of iron during the eleven-hour stretch, or five and one-half tons per man per hour.

Jack Casement bristled and said his men could do better. But Crocker had picked his moment well; there weren't ten miles of track left to be laid. Casement wired UP President Durant for permission to tear up UP track for a rematch, but Durant refused, and Crocker's record went unbeaten until the era of mechanized track laying.

By May 7, the road was done. The last two rails joining the lines together would be laid by dignitaries on the tenth. Thousands of workers were paid off and let go. Many left at once, for the East or for California, but others stayed to watch the history that would be made on Monday. CP President Leland Stanford and a trainload of luminaries from Sacramento arrived on the weekend in a driving rain, but there was no sign of the train from Omaha.

For good reason. The UP delegation had been kidnapped and were being held for "ransom." On the sixth, as the dignitary-laden train passed through Piedmont, a hundred miles east of Promontory, it was waylaid by a mob of angry tie-cutters who had not received their final paycheck. Until they were paid, they announced, UP President Durant and his friends weren't going anywhere. Throughout the day on the seventh, the top brass of the company waited in Piedmont while back in New York, Oakes Ames tried to figure out how to cable money to the disgruntled lumberjacks. The cash finally arrived that evening, the men were paid off, and the embarrassed dignitaries were given a rousing send-off early the following morning.

Rain fell all day Saturday and Sunday. Stanford had his train backed to Monument Point with its splendid views of the Great Salt Lake. Sunday night the sky was clear.

Monday. A crowd of five hundred had gathered by noon; journalists, railway officials, newly unemployed Chinese and Irish railroad workers, soldiers from Fort Douglas, the curious from Salt Lake, two bands, and a handful of Promontory strumpets. The two trains approached each other over the last few yards of respective roads. To the roar of the crowd, Durant and Stanford stepped down and tramped through the mud to shake hands. Crocker greeted Grenville Dodge. Just after 2:00, Dodge signaled for silence. Four Chinese, decked out in denim pantaloons and jackets, their pigtails specially braided and tied, trotted up with the last rail. As they approached, a waiting photographer shouted, "Shoot!" and the startled Chinese dropped the rail and bolted. They were eventually rounded up, and the ceremony continued.

The rail was lowered into place and spiked to all but the last tie, a silver-coated piece of laurel brought by Stanford. The final spike was solid gold, melted down from twenty-dollar goldpieces, costing $413. The names of the chief officers of both companies were engraved on its four sides. A telegraph wire was attached to it to allow for the simultaneous transmission of the final blows to every town and city in the country. The spike was fitted into its hole, and Stanford raised a silver-headed maul to strike the first blow. By prearranged signal, the telegraph operator at the scene tapped three *dots* over the wire: the next taps would correspond exactly with the final blows to the the last spike in the last rail of the transcontinental railroad.

Stanford brought the maul down. And missed. (The telegraph operator supplied the sound anyway.) Durant struck next—and missed as well. Officials from both sides took turns. The golden spike sank slowly into the silver-coated tie. Hats sailed. The crowd cheered. The bands played "America." In Philadelphia, the Liberty Bell pealed. In San Francisco, fire bells tolled, and cannons boomed. In Washington, a magnetic ball dropped from a pole atop the Capitol, igniting a great roar from the assembled throng. Church bells rang out across the nation. "This," said General Dodge, "is the way to India."

The two locomotives uncoupled and inched forward until they

touched. Their engineers climbed out onto the pilot decks, broke a bottle of champagne over each other, and shook hands. Then they backed up their engines, and each drove over the junction. Several Chinese, meanwhile, replaced the silver tie and the gold and silver spikes with normal ones, but souvenir hunters stole "last" ties and "last" spikes as fast as the Chinese could lay them.

Even before the cheering and champagne at Promontory Point, thousands of Chinese and whites began making their way back over the mountains to the coast. But it was a different world from the one they had left to become railroad builders: One out of every four Chinese was now unemployed as well as the more than thirteen thousand whites who had worked on the transcontinental. Already the signs of what became known as the Panic of 1873, the worst depression the country has ever seen, were beginning to set in. In this faltering economy, jobs would be few, laborers a dime a dozen, and resentment against the Chinese would reach fever pitch. The Pacific slope could not begin to absorb the sojourners now pouring out of the Sierra Nevada. Or rather, it might be able to absorb them, but at the expense of whites.

The sojourner's fall from grace was inevitable, caused in part by the deteriorating economy and in part by his own attitude toward his sojourn in America. There had always been about his presence here the distinct smell of opportunism; he did not come to America to stay but to make enough money to be able to leave. Unlike other immigrants who might also have come to prosper, the Oriental did not intend to join the social order or to participate in the building of economic and political systems. He did not intend to contribute, merely to profit.

Nor was the melting-pot ethos to his liking. The sojourner kept strictly to himself, living in transplanted Chinatowns, seldom learning English. Almost none of his money went back into the economy, or into the American economy at any rate. The food he ate came from China, as well as the clothes he wore and the soap he used. Even the rooms he let, in the cities at least, were owned by other Chinese. The sojourner might have been forgiven his opportunism if there had been something in it for the American, but there was not.

At first, the sojourner took jobs no one else wanted: cooking, washing clothes, gardening. But as more Chinese arrived during the 1850s and 1860s, they began to enter a wide variety of new "white" occupations, such as cigar making, all kinds of factory work, even farming. Before long, the sojourner was not simply working alongside

the white man, he was working *instead* of the white man. The reason
was money: Thanks to how he lived, the sojourner could afford to
accept a much lower salary than the white worker and still make a
considerable profit. A typical Chinese lived with eight or nine others
of his kind in a single room in a cheap cardboard lodging house and
spent a total of $8 to $10 a month. The white man, on the other hand,
with a wife and family to support, needed $50 a month to get by. "To
an American," the Manifesto of the Workingman's Party of California
noted, "death is preferable to life on a par with the Chinaman. We
cannot hope to drive the Chinaman out by working cheaper than he
does. None but an enemy would expect it of us, none but an idiot could
hope for success."[14]

Consider, too, who these white men were. They were new to the
coast in most cases, and while some had come to make quick fortunes
in the goldfields, most had more modest hopes. For them it was
enough to escape the oppression of factory work and the drudgery of
day jobs, to leave the overcrowded cities of the East with their
depressed salaries and dwindling opportunities, and start over,
however humbly, in California. For men such as these to find economic
oppression alive and well on the Pacific slope and to find, moreover,
that even this scaled-down version of the California dream was being
underbid at every turn by "moon-eyed, rat eating pagans"—this was
almost past enduring.

And there was, inevitably, the question of race prejudice. Even if
he had learned English, patronized American businesses, spent from
his precious pile—even if he had come to stay—the sojourner was still
an Oriental, rather more different from the other immigrants than they
were from one another. His looks and his inscrutable ways may not
have made integration impossible, but they did make it immensely
more complicated.

Strictly speaking, of course, the sojourner was not the villain; the
man who employed him, who chose him over the American, was.
"The Chinaman is here because his presence pays," a Sacramento
paper editorialized, "and he will remain and continue to increase so
long as there is money in him. We will not [send him home] so long as
the pockets into which the profits of his labor flow continue to be those
appertaining to our [own] pantaloons."[15] If nameless, faceless
industrialists in New York and London and wealthy merchant princes
in San Francisco stopped hiring the Chinese, the Chinese would stop
coming.

But if he was not the villain of the piece, the sojourner was nevertheless a willing accomplice. He knew of the storm gathering around him, the risks he took in coming to America to play the spoiler, and he came anyway, for he knew as well that his benefactors, if they needed him enough, would somehow contrive to protect him.

The anti-Chinese forces, which by 1870 included the vast majority of the working class of the Pacific slope, had two weapons in their arsenal: violence and the vote. While they would turn to violence in the end, in the beginning the vote was the weapon of choice. As the largest constituency in California by far, the labor bloc filled the state legislature with its handmaidens, and the legislators, not surprisingly, precipitated a cascade of anti-Chinese laws. These laws outdid each other in their extremes of unconstitutionality, as every legislator who voted for them was well aware, but it was simply not expedient to oppose them. Let the courts be the bearers of bad tidings.

First there were the taxes. The Foreign Miners Tax required every foreigner engaged in mining to pay a monthly tax of $20 (or two-thirds the average salary for a sojourner). This tax had a curious result. Because of it, so many Chinese left mining and became merchants and shopkeepers that white merchants and shopkeepers complained vigorously and managed to get the tax lowered to $4. Beyond that, however, the legislature dared not go, for during the years 1850–1870 revenue from the Foreign Miners Tax accounted for one-half of all state income, 85 percent coming from the Chinese.

For those Chinese not in mining there was the Fishing Tax. And for all others there was something called the Chinese Police Tax, $4 a month, required of "each member of the Mongolian race over eighteen who is not engaged in fishing or mining." There was a Laundry Tax, too, with a curious sliding scale: You paid $2 quarterly if you used a one-horse vehicle to collect and deliver laundry, $4 for a two-horse vehicle, and $15 if, like nearly every Chinese in the business, you used no vehicle at all.

And there was a Hospital Tax, even though no Chinese were allowed in city hospitals. The Chinese in San Francisco got around this exclusion by raising $75,000 to build their own hospital, only to be informed by the board of supervisors that the city could not permit the operation of a hospital staffed with Chinese managers and physicians.

But the Golden Mountain, even after taxes, was still profitable, so other legislation followed, pursuing the sojourner relentlessly into every corner of his life and work. The Page Law struck at coolieism by making it a felony to import a Chinese without his consent. Another law assessed shipowners $50 a head for anyone on board "incompetent to become a citizen"—citizenship a status denied the Chinese. The Queue Ordinance stipulated that every male prisoner in California— many of whom were Chinese in the wake of all the new laws—must shave his head to within one inch of his scalp. The queue was the symbol of a sojourner's membership in and submission to the Manchu regime; without it, he could not return to China.

The Chinese were excluded from public schools, from jobs on public works, denied the right to own land, to testify in court against Caucasians (Indians and blacks were also denied this right), to have special police (after the San Francisco police proved unable or unwilling to protect the residents of Chinatown), and it was a misdemeanor for "any officer, director, manager, member, stockholder, clerk, agent, servant, attorney, employee or contractor of any corporation [to employ] in any manner or capacity any Chinese or Mongolians." Further:

> The Chinese were arrested for carrying vegetable baskets on the sidewalk, for discharging firearms, for having theatrical performances in certain hours and for beating gongs at such performances. Hoodlums demanded cigars of the Chinese peddler and then had him arrested for having unstamped cigars in his possession. The poll tax collectors stationed themselves at the ferry landing in San Francisco and compelled the Chinese who lived in Oakland to pay their tax a second time. The Board of Health refused to allow them to send the bodies of their dead back to China.[16]

And the Cubic Air Ordinance, aimed at San Francisco's Chinatown, required lodging houses to provide five hundred cubic feet of airspace for each adult lodger. So many landlords were arrested and detained the day the law went into effect that the jail itself was in violation of the ordinance.

The anti-Chinese forces gathered strength throughout the 1850s and 1860s. At election time, "anti-coolie" clubs invited candidates to appear and express their views on the Chinese question. Many politicians changed parties, from Republican to Democrat, to be on the right side of the issue, and one even won the statehouse in the process. "Asia," Governor Stanford declared (in yet another flip-flop), "with her numberless millions sends to our shores the dregs of her population. It is clear that the settlement among us of an inferior race is to be discouraged by every legitimate means."[17]

With the completion of the transcontinental, the anti-Chinese movement entered a new phase. Immigration from the Celestial

Kingdom reached near-record proportions in the three years 1868–1870, raising the sojourner's profile at an especially awkward moment. In July 1870, the anti-Chinese forces organized a massive demonstration in San Francisco. The first of many, the affair was sponsored by two large labor groups: the Knights of St. Crispin and the Plumbers and Carpenters Eight Hour League. Workers marched through the streets by the hundreds, cheering and carrying banners: No Servile Labor Shall Pollute Our Land, Women's Rights, No More Chinese Chambermaids, The Chinese Must Go. The next day, the heads of the famous Six Companies, the Chinese organization responsible for recruiting most of the Chinese in America, received a letter from the protest's organizers: "We do not consider it just or safe to the Chinese," the letter warned, "to continue coming to the United States."[18]

This was something new. The anti-Chinese forces, more organized than before, were no longer preaching economic harassment but exclusion, and their argument was not that a sojourn on the Golden Mountain might not be profitable but that it might not be safe. Just over a year later, on the night of October 24, 1871, on Nigger Alley in the Chinese quarter of Los Angeles, they were proven spectacularly right. On that night, a mob attacked and murdered twenty-three sojourners, and the anti-Chinese movement in America, for the first time, crossed over the threshold of violence.

Nigger Alley was in a notoriously seamy quarter of the city. Thieves, outlaws, Mexican bandits, fugitives from justice of every ilk haunted the shabby lodging houses and rundown bars, committing, on the average, twenty to thirty murders a month. "Some of the greatest desperadoes on the Pacific Coast were to be found there."[19] Chinatown itself consisted of a single block of one-story, whitewashed, windowless adobe buildings, fully two-thirds of which were reputedly brothels. Nearly every night, there was a stabbing or a shooting.

"The worst night Los Angeles has ever known"[20] started as a fight over a whore, one Ya Hit. Young and attractive, Ya Hit was purchased for $2,500 by Sam Yuen, the owner of one of two rival companies in Los Angeles. Sometime thereafter, she ran away, or was stolen, and came into the possession of Yo Hing, owner of the other company. Sam Yuen schemed to get her back by having a warrant issued for her arrest on the charge that she had stolen jewelry belonging to him. Ya Hit was brought into court and arraigned, and bail was set. Sam paid the bail and thereby repossessed the young woman.

Yo Hing, "who in every way sustained the national reputation of his race for ways that are dark,"[21] went Sam one better: He somehow contacted the woman and persuaded her to marry him; Ya Hit changed hands yet again. Sam retaliated by offering a reward of $1,000 for the scalp of Yo Hing and sent to San Francisco for two professional executioners, whereupon a state of war was declared between the two companies and their retainers.

On Monday morning, October 23, as he walked down Nigger Alley, Yo Hing was fired upon by two gunmen hiding in a Chinese store. Two of the bullets missed, but a third pierced his coat. Yo Hing swore out a warrant against the two gunmen, and they swore one out against him. All three were arrested, released on bail, and ordered to appear in court the next morning.

Throughout the following day, as the case was being heard in court, preparations for a showdown went forward in Chinatown. The Chinese bought up all the guns they could find, exchanged threats and warnings, and boarded up their homes. Late in the afternoon, imported toughs arrived by steamer from San Francisco. Los Angeles police were warned of possible trouble, and mounted officers were ordered to the vicinity. At 5:00 P.M. court adjourned, and the case was held over to the following day. Both parties returned to Chinatown.

At 5:30, Officer Bildermain heard shooting coming from the Chinese quarter and hurried to the scene. While the officer was trying to stop the gunfight, Yo Hing shot him in the shoulder. Bildermain cried out for help. Robert Thompson, an old resident of the neighborhood, rushed to his aid and was also shot, just above the heart. He was taken around the corner to Wallweber's drugstore where he died an hour later.

Meanwhile, an angry crowd of the area's other citizens began to gather, and the Chinese ran in off the street. Many took refuge in a long one-story building in the middle of the block and started firing at the mob. Others, including Yo Hing and most of the hired toughs, bolted through back streets and alleys, and hid out in nearby orange groves and vineyards. Still others jammed the nearby jail.

The mob returned the fire on the Chinese stronghold, riddling it with bullets, and the Chinese inside answered round for round. One frightened sojourner sprang from the building and tried to escape across the street, but he was cut down almost at once. He was followed a few minutes later by a second Chinese who dashed into the street brandishing an axe. Before the crowd could fire, two policemen grabbed the man and marched off toward the jail. The mob closed in on the prisoner, demanding that he be hung, and one rioter tried to stab the Chinese in the back. He missed and struck one of the policemen in the hand instead. The instant the wounded officer let go of the prisoner, the mob snatched him away, dragged him off to Tomlinson's corral on New High Street, and hung him.

Some of the rioters broke away to loot the abandoned houses along the street, rifling every room in Chinatown before the night was over. They ransacked trunks and boxes, smashed open locked cases, and spilled their contents into the street, searching everywhere for the sojourners' legendary piles.

The crowd besieging the stronghold tried three or four times to set the place on fire. Finally, around 8:00 P.M., guns blazing, the mob rushed the building. Several rioters jumped onto the roof and started hacking at it with axes. When they broke through, they fired down on the Chinese huddled inside. Others, out in front, battered in the door and burst in on the startled defenders. Several were shot on the spot, and the rest were hauled into the street.

Now the mob went wild. Methodically robbing each victim first, they threw ropes around their necks and dragged them along the stone street until they found a place to string them up. A few sojourners died before they could be hung. Three dangled from a straining gutter. Three others swung from an awning, helped into their fall by a boy of ten who stood on the roof and pulled the victims into position. Four more were hung from a wagon. And four others were strung up next to their compatriot on the gateway arch at Tomlinson's corral. At one point, the mob ran out of rope, whereupon a woman saved the day by offering her clothesline.

The most prominent victim was Gene Tung, a Chinese doctor respected by all who knew him, including many in the white community. In both English and Spanish, he pleaded for his life, offering his captors all his wealth, some $3,000, if they would spare him. They took the money and strung him up anyway, stripping off all his fine clothes and cutting off his fingers to get at his valuable rings.

By 9:30 P.M., when Sheriff Burns and a force of twenty-five local citizens finally showed up, the carnage was over. Some fifteen corpses dangled in the moonlight, and several other mutilated bodies lay strewn about the street. Authorities later determined that only one or two of the dead had actually been part of the dispute that led to the riot; the rest died because they were Chinese. " 'The Chinese Must Go!' was the watchword that night," one journalist wrote, "but no Chinaman was given the chance."[22]

Legitimate anti-Chinese interests had nothing to do with the slaughter on Nigger Alley and joined in the chorus of outrage, but all the same a precedent had been set. As anti-Chinese sentiment on the West Coast spread and deepened in the years after the Los Angeles riot, the specter of that calamity lent a new urgency to calls for action and a solution to the "Chinese question."

By 1876, the tide had turned inexorably against the sojourner. That winter brought the lowest rainfall in twenty-five years to the Pacific slope; California's wheat crop was ruined, cattle died by the thousands, the fruit industry nearly collapsed, and, by coincidence, mining receipts, California's major source of income after agriculture, were the lowest ever. Wages plummeted, and unemployment, already high in the wake of the depression, was rampant. In San Francisco alone, there were ten thousand jobless.

With poor timing, more Chinese chose the period 1873–1876 to emigrate to America than any comparable period before or since, and the sojourners continued to venture, with increasing success, beyond their traditional occupations as miners, house servants, and launderers. By 1880, for example, more than one-third of California's farm laborers were Chinese.

In such fertile soil, the anti-Chinese movement thrived. Labor and other anti-Chinese groups were active in the state elections of 1876, helping the Democrats win a resounding victory over the Republicans, who were decidedly more moderate on the issue of foreign labor. The following spring, the mayor of San Francisco named a twelve-man committee to investigate and document the evils of Chinese immigration in that city and carry its findings to Washington. A mass meeting took place at the end of March to give the committee a proper send-off, and Governor Irwin was on hand to sound the theme of this stepped-up campaign against the sojourner: "It is not, fellow citizens, a question of morals, of social conditions, of political economy.... The subversion of our civilization is involved. If the influx of this race continues, they become the laborers of our country."[23]

There was renewed violence as well. In June, miners attacked one thousand Chinese in Truckee and drove them from the town. Five Chinese tenant farmers on the Lemm Ranch were killed, their bodies and cabins burned. A favorite pastime in Tucson was to rope a sojourner to the back of a steer and run him out of town. In Tombstone, cowboys cut cards for the honor of expelling Chinese. The worst harassment was in San Francisco where Chinese were attacked in the streets, stoned at the docks, and pulled from moving streetcars and beaten. "We don't mind hearing of a Chinese being killed now and then," wrote a Montana reporter, "but it has been coming too thick of late. Don't kill them unless they deserve it, but when they do—why kill 'em lots."[24]

The presidents of the Six Companies pleaded with the mayor of San Francisco: "Large gatherings of the idle and irresponsible element of the population of this city are nightly addressed in the open streets by speakers who use the most violent and incendiary language, threatening in plainest terms to burn and pillage the Chinese quarter and kill our people. . . . We appeal to you to protect us. . . . We should regret to have the good name of this Christian civilization tarnished by the riotous proceedings of its own citizens against the 'Chinese heathen.' "[25]

Now the pace quickened. In October, in response to the visit by the mayor's committee to Washington, a joint special committee of the U.S. Congress traveled to San Francisco to hold hearings on the Chinese question. In a sense, the fact of the committee's visit was nearly as important as its subsequent findings, for it symbolized the growing influence the states along the Pacific slope were beginning to exercise in Washington. Taken together, the senators and representatives from the coast comprised an eleven-man voting bloc in Congress (and held 11 electoral votes); if the constituents of this important group were concerned about the Chinese, then Congress would have to be too.

Scores of witnesses appeared before the joint committee to spell out the case against the Chinese (and almost none appeared in his defense). A doctor and a health officer declared that the Chinese were responsible for bringing leprosy and smallpox to California. Another witness testified that the sojourner was "morally and intellectually incapable of understanding the priviliged rights of citizenship," and a third witness noted that the Chinese were "a people who have not the least consciousness of truth and veracity . . . and are incapable of attaining the state of civilization the Caucasion is capable of."[26] Two committee members, it turned out, were also honorary vice-presidents of the Anti-Chinese Union. The committee's report, published the following February, was all the anti-Chinese forces could have hoped for: Its principal recommendation was for the exclusion of Chinese immigrants from America.

Later that year, Congress was debating its first exclusion bill, the so-called Fifteen Passenger Act. That particular bill, though passed by the Congress, was vetoed by President Hayes, who cited among his reasons certain treaty obligations to the Chinese and his concern for the safety of American merchants and missionaries working in China.

To soften the blow and demonstrate that in fact he was on the right side of the issue, Hayes announced that he was asking George Seward, minister to China, to begin negotiations at once with the Chinese government for the restriction of immigration.

The negotiations dragged on for over a year, and Seward was eventually recalled and replaced by a three-man commission. The commissioners finished their work in November 1880, finally persuading the Chinese to agree to language that conceded to the United States the power to "regulate, limit, or suspend . . . but not absolutely prohibit" the immigration of laborers. The Chinese insisted, however, that workers already in the country, or who came before the new treaty provision was officially ratified by both governments, be allowed to stay.

When the news was announced, Congress was inundated by a score of restriction bills. Supporters eventually rallied around the version introduced by Senator Miller, which provided for a twenty-year suspension of immigration. A fierce, often hysterical fight followed. Petitions and memorials poured into Washington from the coast. The railroad lobby strongly opposed the bill, calling on the president to honor America's historic commitment to the principle of the equality of the races. Senator Hoar of Massachusetts found the bill "degrading." Senator Miller, the bill's author, was no less restrained. "The failure of this bill," he said, "would be to commission all the traffickers in human flesh to ply their infamous trade without impediment and empty the teeming, seething slave pens of China upon the soil of California."[27] On May 6, 1882, after prevailing upon Congress to change the period of suspension from twenty years to ten, the president signed the bill.

But suspension wasn't exclusion. Nor, as it turned out, was it even suspension. The bill the president signed was deeply flawed, thanks in large part to effective lobbying by the railroads and business interests, which left the new act riddled with loopholes. To begin with, the new law did not prevent the immigration of Chinese coming from countries other than China, such as the Philippines, Hawaii, or Cuba—all of which had large concentrations of Chinese labor. Chinese in transit to or from other countries were likewise allowed into U.S. ports, from which many of them quietly disappeared. Certain classes of immigrants, such as teachers, merchants, and travelers, were exempt from the restriction, and a brisk business soon sprang up in the forging and selling of certificates that allowed such persons to enter the country legally. Sojourners already in the country were also issued certificates, which, when they sailed back to China for good, they passed on to their brethren waiting to come. Hundreds of Chinese sailed to Canada and were smuggled over the border. "Federal authorities along [Puget] Sound," the Salt Lake *Herald* reported, "hardly make a pretext of stopping Mongols from crossing that border into Washington Territory from British Columbia. [The restriction] act is a dead letter."[28]

Moreover, in anticipation of the new law, more Chinese immigrated to America in 1882 than in any other single year, over forty thousand, or one-third the number already resident. The census of 1890 found more Chinese in the country than ten years earlier.

Yet Congress and the president *had* acted, and acted decisively in their view, boldly breaking with one hundred years of tradition and declaring that America was no longer a land of open immigration. They did what had to be done, they all agreed, but having done so, no one was anxious to revisit the issue any time soon. As far as Washington was concerned, the Chinese question had been settled.

In truth, the Chinese question was now more unsettled than ever. With a record number of sojourners now living on the coast and the anti-Chinese movement reeling from the gift of "suspension," hostility and tension had never been so high. In the present climate, only extreme measures—violence foremost among them—seemed likely to be able to break the impasse and precipitate a resolution of the crisis. It was not surprising, then, that when a group of miners in an obscure coal camp in southwestern Wyoming attacked the local Chinatown, the sparks from the incident touched off a series of anti-Chinese explosions the length and breadth of the Pacific slope and determined, once and for all, the future of the Chinese in America.

2

Salvation

*I do not now recall a single one of the many journeys I have made
in all sections of the territory during which outcroppings of coal
were not seen. Throughout a southern belt of fifty to one-hundred
miles, traversed by the Union Pacific Railroad, it shows itself
almost constantly.*

—GOV. JOHN HOYT

The coal camp went by the name of Rock Springs. The original spring bubbled out through a cleft in the rocks a few steps from the Killpecker, a tributary of Bitter Creek. It was discovered, the story goes, by a Pony Express rider fleeing a band of marauding Indians. In 1862, Ben Holladay, owner of the Overland Trail Company, built a station beside the spring and hired two Scottish immigrants to manage it.

Archibald and Duncan Blair, disappointed gold seekers from Rothesay, Scotland, added a stockade to hold the four- and six-horse teams they supplied the Overland, built a trading post and a wayside inn, threw a stone bridge over the Killpecker, and built themselves a sturdy stone cabin, complete with rifle holes every twelve feet for shooting at Indians and bandits. They hired Becky Thomas to cook antelope steak and brew thick prairie coffee for the dust-caked passengers, sired children by Shoshoni squaws, and all the while kept their eyes on the big prize.

That prize, a giant vein of coal, lay three miles south of the station, on the other side of Bitter Creek. With the Union Pacific slated to pass through this area in two years, the brothers Blair were about to become coal miners and, with any luck, net themselves a tidy fortune. They were right on two counts: the railroad would indeed pass through the heart of the Bitter Creek depression, and there was a fortune to be made from coal. But it wouldn't be made by Archie and Duncan.

The story of Rock Springs begins one morning in early September 1852 when Captain Howard Stansbury of the U.S. Topographical Engineers received a change of orders. Stansbury, who had just completed a two-year survey of the Great Salt Lake Valley and was preparing to depart for the East, was ordered instead to hire a competent guide and proceed into southern Wyoming to investigate possible routes and fuel sources for a national railroad. He hired the best guide in the business, mountain man Jim Bridger, and struck out from Salt Lake in early September. Bridger led him up the Green River, through spectacular Red Canyon, and out onto the western reaches of what was known as the Red Desert. Here, where Bitter Creek meets Green River, the party turned east. "At a point 13 miles from the mouth of Bitter Creek," Stansbury noted in his journal on September 14, "we found a bed of bituminous coal cropping out of the north bluff of the valley, with every indication of its being quite abundant."[1]

The captain and his men spent all day on the fifteenth exploring "this remarkable depression," and then broke camp the following morning, continuing eastward: "Sandstone cliffs bound the valley on the north side, in which I observed a stratum of coal which was exposed for a hundred yards and was at least ten feet in thickness. During the whole day's march this mineral was met with in every favorable locality and in quantities apparently without limit."[2]

In fact, Stansbury had found one of the richest coal deposits in the world, twice as large as the more famous Pennsylvania fields, over nineteen million acres in all. In one reckoning, the U.S. Geological Survey estimated the total at 424 billion tons, while still other geologists set the figure at 700 billion or even a trillion tons. In 1891, the Union Pacific calculated that the mineral wealth of Wyoming alone, most of it coal, could more than pay off the national debt. "In the course of time," the railroad noted, "these little known resources will release multitudinous forms of energies and vitalizing forces that will dwarf the sum total now being generated within a dozen of the most highly industrialized valleys of the world. No comparisons are possible for the Green River valley."[3]

Stansbury's findings, published in 1853, created a sensation. For thirty years, rich industrialists, powerful politicians, and at least three presidents had dreamed of a continent-spanning railroad. By the 1850s, the iron rails were halfway, at the eastern edge of the Missouri

River, stopped cold by the yawning wastes of Nebraska, Wyoming, and Utah (labeled on maps as the Great American Desert) and the mighty wall of the Rockies. California called, but the more than fifteen hundred miles from Omaha to Sacramento posed a formidable challenge. Except for Salt Lake City and Denver, the region was largely uninhabited (if you didn't count the Indians, and no one did), and beyond that there were no trees. Even if you could build a railroad across this pitiless waste, what would you use for fuel? Without wood, you would have to use coal, and unless high-quality coal could be found in abundance west of the Missouri, it would have to be shipped in from the East, and the cost of that was unthinkable. And for years the argument ended there, foundering on the rock of fuel.

But Stansbury's report changed everything. The Wyoming deposits, the Union Pacific later declared, were "a discovery of almost incalculable value to the company and to the country along the line of the road.... The fuel question has been one which it was feared would be hard to meet in the far West, but the discovery of this coal field has solved the problem."[4]

But there were two things wrong with Captain Stansbury's coal: It didn't belong to the government, and there was no easy way to get to it. The latter difficulty was resolved by a fortuitous accident, but the former proved more intractable and in the end, was resolved by tragedy.

The problem was the Shoshoni. While the proposed new railroad passed through the heart of Indian Territory, most of the tribes, by the terms of the Treaty of Fort Laramie, had withdrawn behind government-established boundaries and turned control of the better part of the High Plains over to the Great Father in Washington. The Shoshoni, however, whose homeland in the Green River valley sat directly astride the route and included the Wyoming coal deposits, had neither signed the infamous treaty nor, in the decade prior to the beginning of the construction of the new railroad, given the government any cause to bring them to the negotiating table and conclude a separate peace.

Such exemplary conduct, sustained against all odds throughout the tumultuous 1850s, as all around them tribe after tribe rose up in wrath against the great immigrant tide en route to California, picking the Indian hunting grounds clean of feed and game—such conduct on the part of the Shoshoni was not accidental; rather, it was the deliberate policy of the tribe, a calculated gamble conceived and masterminded by one of the greatest of all Indian leaders, Chief Washakie. Washakie,

Chief Washakie. (Photograph from The Thomas Gilcrease Institute of American History and Art, Tulsa, Oklahoma)

who ascended to the leadership of the tribe in the late 1840s, never forgot the sight of his first firearm, which he had encountered as a young man at the campsite of a fur trapper. "We'll never prosper by fighting men who can make that," he declared, and thereafter nonviolence became the cornerstone of his fifty-year rule, a near-constant struggle to steer a delicate middle course between the increasingly rapacious demands of the white man on the one hand and the needs of his people on the other. At stake, as it was for all the tribes in the wake of the opening of the West, was nothing less than the continued existence, as a social and cultural entity, of his people, which in turn was inseparably linked to and embodied within the starkly beautiful landscapes of their tribal homeland in the Green River valley and the Wind River Mountains of western Wyoming. Washakie was betting that the surest way to secure that homeland was not to give anyone, and especially not the white man, an excuse to take it.

For fourteen years, from his ascendancy in 1848 until the spring of 1862, the policy worked. Under the circumstances—this was arguably one of the most difficult periods in the history of the Shoshoni nation—it was a remarkable accomplishment. In 1849, gold was discovered in California, and overnight the High Plains was transformed into a great turnpike to the Pacific. In 1849 alone, 40,000 people crossed the continent. One traveler, moving east against the tide, reported passing 4,000 wagons of 4 people each in only four hours. An observer at Fort Kearney, Nebraska, tallied 800 wagons and 10,000 oxen past that post in a single day. The next year, 1850, 60,000 gold seekers and 90,000 stock made the crossing, appropriating as they went all the feed between Fort Laramie and Fort Bridger, a 400-mile-long, 5-mile-wide swath of desolation across the entire state of Wyoming, "as smooth as a bare floor swept by the winds."[5] With the grass went the buffalo, antelope, and deer who ate it to live, and with the game went the Indian way of life. In the Shoshoni tongue, the Oregon Trail was known as the River of Destruction.

One day Father de Smet, a Jesuit missionary, took some Shoshoni out to look at the great migration. "They fancied," he wrote, "that an immense void must [be left] in the land of the rising sun." When the good father assured the Indians that this flood of humanity pouring out of the East, a few hours' worth equal to the whole Shoshoni nation, "was in no way perceived in the land of the whites," they could not comprehend.[6] "There seemed no end," Washakie later noted, "to the hordes of white men."[7]

The pressure on the Shoshoni, hence on Washakie, was particularly acute, thanks to an accident of geography. While the emigrant tide approached the mountains by a number of trails, all the northern routes converged at the same place, that great funnel through the Rockies known as South Pass. Beyond the pass, in the Green River valley, the routes split again, south toward Salt Lake and the California goldfields, north toward Oregon. South Pass, that moment where the wide River of Destruction was walled into a narrow, raging torrent, lay at the southern end of the Wind River Range, in the heart of the Shoshoni homeland.

A lesser man than Washakie could not have held his tribe in check in the face of such an onslaught, and even he succeeded only because of his reputation, won before he became chief, as a fearless warrior. He once trailed a Blackfoot raiding party nearly five hundred miles, from the Green River to the Missouri, to recover some stolen horses (and brought the raiders' scalps back for good measure). "As a young man," he observed later, "I delighted in war. When my tribe was at peace, I would wander off, sometimes alone, in search of an enemy. I am ashamed to speak of those years for I killed a great many Indians."[8]

One evening near the end of the 1850s, as his policies came under increasing opposition, Washakie overheard a group of young braves calling him weak and cowardly, speculating about who might replace him. The next morning, telling no one, the chief slipped out of camp before dawn and rode east into enemy Sioux and Arapaho country where he stayed for several weeks. The night of his return, he called a council of his warriors. Washakie sat in the middle of his tepee on an elevated seat covered in the skins of panther, bear, and mountain lion. The elders of the tribe sat in a circle around him, and the younger braves stood at the back. A fire gave off the only light, its smoke filling the tent with a faint bluish haze. When all had gathered, the chief rose as if to speak, but instead he pulled seven scalps out from under his robe and tossed them on the ground before the astonished assembly. "Let him [sic] who can do a greater feat than this claim the chieftainship," he declared. "Let him who would take my place count as many scalps."[9] And with that, the sixty-year-old chief strode briskly out of the tepee . Though he would live and rule for another forty years, to the dawn of the twentieth century, his position was never again challenged.

Washakie was a big man for an Indian, over six feet tall, weighing nearly 250 pounds. "He was a great eater," General O. O. Howard said of him, "and it was always a mystery to me how one Indian could eat so much. He ate very politely, but it was like a giant taking his food."[10] But there was no mystery about it to Washakie: "I like meat," he said. "I like bread, I like vegetables. I am big, so I eat much."[11] Yet he was remarkably trim and muscular and kept his perfect form and erect posture all his life. He was lighter-skinned than most Shoshoni and had beautiful teeth and long flowing white hair. He usually wore a foxskin robe and went bareheaded. In his last years, however, he took to covering his head to remind himself of the shame one of his sons had brought upon the family (and the tribe) by getting shot in a barroom brawl. His son, he said, "died like an Arapaho," that is, like an Indian who drank.[12]

Washakie lived simply, eschewing in later years the fine wood-frame house the Great Father provided for him, preferring his tepee instead. He found the house "heap cold" and quartered his horses in it. Horses, in fact, were his passion, and upon becoming chief, he outlawed the practice of blinding the animals in the right eye to make it easier to approach and rope them as they grazed.

When Washakie died on February 2, 1900, he was buried with full military honors, the only Indian ever accorded such a privilege, and his funeral procession, which stretched for a mile and a half, was the longest in Wyoming history.

In the spring of 1862, a group of hotheads and malcontents among the Shoshoni decided they had had enough of Washakie's passivity and broke away from the tribe to throw in their lot with Chief Bear Hunter and the Bannock. Not long after, on April 14, groups of renegade Shoshoni and Bannock attacked a number of stage stations across a two-hundred-mile stretch of the Overland Trail in western Wyoming. They slew the black chef at the Split Rock Station, set the buildings on fire, and ran off with the stock. The stages were hit as well, coaches upended and burned, passengers and crew robbed and menaced, and more than sixty horses stolen. Travelers and drivers made their way on foot to the nearest stations—and found smoking ruins.

The attacks were the provocation the government had been waiting for to subdue the Shoshoni and, by the terms of the peace, appropriate their lands. But before the Great Father in Washington could dictate the terms of the peace, he first had to win the war.

That job went to Colonel Patrick Connor and the Third California Infantry. Connor, a veteran of the Mexican and Seminole wars, had moved to California in 1850 and resigned his commission. When the Civil War broke out, he was pressed back into service as a colonel, but he was on the wrong side of the country from the fighting. Anxious to see combat and win a promotion, he was surprised and pleased to receive orders in April 1862 to proceed at once to Utah Territory to put down an Indian revolt. As it happened, the particular assignment suited him well: "Indians," he once told General Grenville Dodge, "should be hunted like wolves."

The colonel took his time getting to Salt Lake. Summer was the worst period for making a forced march across the sunbaked wastes of the Great Basin and the Utah desert, but the situation along the emigrant trail was getting worse by the week. Encouraged by the lack of any retaliation from the army, the renegade Shoshoni and Bannock were plundering and marauding at will throughout western Wyoming, eastern Utah, and into Idaho, finally obliging the commissioner of

Indian Affairs in Washington to issue a general proclamation warning travelers of the hostilities. Ben Holladay, owner of the Overland Trail Company, ordered the route moved south (the Rock Springs station was founded at this moment) and made vigorous complaints to the postmaster general about the dangerous, unstable situation. The superintendent of Indian Affairs in Salt Lake cabled the commissioner in Washington to prevail upon the War Department to urge Colonel Connor to pick up his pace, reporting that some two thousand Bannock and Shoshoni were now on the warpath. Finally, in August, four months after he set out, Connor arrived in the Mormon capital.

Suddenly the Indians were on their best behavior, denying Connor the excuse he needed to launch an offensive. But one was soon arranged. One night in December, some government livestock disappeared from the fort where Connor and the Third California were billeting. Connor sent a small force under Major McGary to retrieve the missing animals. McGary captured four Indians but failed to locate any stock. Connor sent word to Bear Hunter that unless the animals were returned, the Indians would be executed. When there was no reply, the prisoners were killed. Bear Hunter took up the fight, pulling Indian women and children into the mountains out of danger and announcing that any white man who set foot north of Bear River would be shot.

Connor marched north in force, with four companies and two howitzers. He found Bear Hunter and his band at their camp just inside Idaho and dispatched a handful of troops to trick the Indians into attacking in strength. The ploy worked, and Connor then brought up the main body of his cavalry. Pressing a large band of warriors deep into a narrow ravine, the colonel sprang his trap. He positioned the howitzers on either side of the ravine's mouth and sent word to Major McGary, hiding with a large force at the far end of the cul-de-sac, to attack. The startled Indians wheeled round and fled back the way they had come, straight into the howitzers' deadly cross fire. Shoshoni and Bannock bodies were piled five- and eight-deep. The army lost fourteen men. Connor was promoted to brigadier general. The black chef at the Split Rock stage station, the sole casualty of the Overland affair, had been avenged.

While only a handful of Shoshoni had fought the war, the entire tribe were made victims of the peace. Washakie, who had denounced the revolt and immediately banished the renegades, was summoned to Fort Bridger the summer after the Bear River massacre to sign a treaty. The terms were all he had feared, reserving to the government "the right to use the lands of the Shoshoni for roads and travel, for military and agricultural settlement and for military posts, to establish ferries across rivers and to erect houses and found settlements at stated points from time to time as the country might develop, and to operate a telegraph and overland stage line as well as a railroad."[13]

The Shoshoni, in a familiar feature of such treaties, were promised an annual payment, in goods, of $20,000. That amount, in an equally familiar gesture, was subsequently reduced to $10,000 by Congress and later that year reduced even further when the government, negotiating other treaties in the area, promised a third tribe a share of the Shoshoni-Bannock annuity. Goods were so scarce that winter, the proud Washakie took the stagecoach to Salt Lake City to beg the government for food and clothing.

Even worse lay ahead for the Shoshoni. After five years of trying to hold his people together on the meager largesse of the government, Washakie was called back to Fort Bridger to sign another treaty, one which officially designated certain portions of the Wind River Range (those portions the government had no use for) a Shoshoni reservation. In its wisdom, the government later decided to give part of the reservation to the Arapaho, the Shoshoni's near neighbors and sworn enemies.

The series of betrayals broke the old chief's heart. While many braves stayed on the reservation, many others, especially the young, the would-be inheritors of the tribe's traditions, drifted into Salt Lake looking for work, often "getting washed" (baptized) by the Mormons as a result. Others, without jobs or prospects, became vagrants, living off the generosity of the city, the stereotypes in many instances of the drunken Indian.

At yet another treaty ceremony in the late 1870s, Washakie, in a famous speech, rehearsed the sad history of his people and the tragic consequences—for all Indians—of the opening of the West. The setting was a large tepee in the shadow of the mountains, where Wyoming Governor Hoyt had come to hear the chief's objections to the proposed treaty. The governor entered on Washakie's arm, and all the elders of the tribe, resplendent in their finest robes, rose "with instinctive politeness," Hoyt later remarked, "for they had never been taught court etiquette." Washakie introduced the governor and then led him to his place on a bearskin.

"I would give anything for a picture of that scene," Hoyt wrote, "the majestic old Washakie, his form as stately as that of Daniel Webster, his face wearing both the dignity and benignity of Washington, his grey locks hanging in profusion down his shoulders, and the thirty superior men of the tribe, with earnest faces, to the right and left and in front of him."[14]

When there was silence, Washakie spoke. "I cannot hope to express to you the half that is in our hearts," he began.

> They are too full for words. The white man, who possesses this whole vast country from sea to sea, who roams over it at pleasure, and lives where he likes, cannot know the cramp we feel in this little spot, with undying remembrance of the fact, which you know as well as we, that every foot of what you proudly call America, not very long ago belonged to the red man. The Great Spirit gave it to us. There was room enough for all his many tribes, and all were happy in their freedom. But the white man had, in ways we know not of, learned some things we had not learned; among them how to make superior tools and terrible weapons, better for war than bows and arrows.
>
> And so, at last, our fathers were steadily driven out, or killed, and we, their sons, but sorry remnants of tribes once mighty, are cornered in little spots of the earth all ours of right—cornered like guilty prisoners and watched by men with guns, who are more than anxious to kill us off.
>
> And your great and mighty government—Oh sir, I hesitate, for I cannot tell the half! It does not protect us in our rights. It leaves us without the promised seed, without tools for cultivating the land, without the schools we so much need for our children. And so, after all we can get by cultivating the land, and by hunting and fishing, we are sometimes nearly starved and half naked, as you see us.
>
> Disappointment; then a deep sadness; then a grief inexpressible; then, at times, a bitterness that makes us think of the rifle, of the knife and the tomahawk, and kindles in our hearts the fires of desperation— that, sir, is the story of our experience, of our wretched lives.[15]

Washakie's policy of nonviolence, made little difference in the end; the way of peace and the way of war both led to the extermination of the Indian and his way of life. War merely did the job more quickly.

The other problem with Captain Stansbury's coal was how to get to it. While the vast deposits of the Green River valley were now in the gift of the government, they were no good to the Union Pacific if the company couldn't lay tracks to them. Of course, the UP could always put in a spur to the coalfields from the nearest point along the line, but the company had something else in mind. By the terms of its charter with the government, for every mile of track the UP laid, it was paid a subsidy and granted a strip of land immediately bordering that mile on either side of the track in a checkerboard pattern. In other words, if the UP could put its tracks through the Green River valley, it would not only be *close* to an inexhaustible source of fuel, but would *own* that fuel outright. In such a scheme, the coalfields of southwestern Wyoming not only solved the problem of fuel, but they might also solve the problem of profits. Indeed, as it turned out, the mines of the Green River valley—and those of Rock Springs in particular—became the salvation of the Union Pacific.

The question throughout 1864 and 1865 as the road inched its way west across Nebraska, was what to do about the Black Hills. This 8,000-foot mountain range sat directly astride the path of the advancing line and appeared to be uncrossable. To get around it, the railroad would have to veer one hundred miles to the north and then follow the route of the old Oregon Trail. But this route not only added forty miles to the length of the line, it also bypassed the Green River coalfields. For eighteen months company surveyors scoured every valley, notch, and pass of the Black Hills, looking in vain for a suitable grade. In the end, another round of "Indian trouble" saved the day.

In 1865, the government began construction of the highly unpopular Bozeman Road, through Sioux, Cheyenne, and Arapaho hunting grounds to the recently discovered Montana goldfields. Three more warlike tribes were not to be found on the High Plains, and the government sent Major General Grenville Dodge to contain the inevitable "hostilities." A competent general, Dodge's real passion was railroad building. Within a year, in fact, he would resign his commission to become chief engineer of the UP. Whenever he could spare time from what became known as the Powder River campaign, Dodge stole into the hills to survey likely routes for the railroad. He studied the Oregon Trail route carefully but did not find it attractive. It was "some forty miles longer than the direct line," he noted, and then added that "on this line there [is] no development of coal."[16]

Dodge knew the obstacle the Black Hills presented, so when the campaign took him to the vicinity, he went "everyday to the summit ... trying to discover some approach from the east that was feasible."[17] On one such excursion, leaving his troops in camp and setting out into the hills with a small guard, he was climbing toward the summit of Cheyenne pass when

we were discovered by Indians, who, at the same time, discovered us. They were between us and our [troops]. I saw our danger and took means immediately to reach the ridge and try to head them off and follow it to where the cavalry could see our signals. We dismounted and started down the ridge, holding the Indians at bay, when they came too close, with our Winchesters. It was nearly night when the troops saw our smoke signals of danger and came to our relief; and in going to the train we followed this ridge out until I discovered it led down to the plains without a break. I then said to my guide that if we saved our scalps, I believed we had found the crossing of the Black Hills.[18]

And so he had. The grade would be steep and the summit the highest elevation of the entire transcontinental railroad, but the mountains had finally been breached.

Back at the rock spring, the Blair brothers waited. Because of the checkerboard pattern of the UP land grants, half of all the property bordering the line still belonged to the government. For a fee, anyone could lease the mineral rights and start a coal company. In 1867, Archie and Duncan did just that, tapping a large seam three miles south of the stage station and thereby opening the first coal mine in Wyoming. Two years later, strewing promise and prosperity in their wake, UP track gangs slapped rails across the Bitter Creek depression—in sight of the Blairs' mine—and pushed off toward Utah. At last the UP had its coalfields, and the Blairs, so they thought, had the makings of their fortune.

Overnight, Wyoming was transformed. Before the coming of the railroad, the state had virtually no white settlers or permanent white settlements. The region "was quite well known to many people, but scarcely anyone had shown any interest in making it his home."[19] Indeed, as late as 1868, Wyoming didn't exist. The area that would become a new territory that year was officially known as Carter and Laramie counties, part of Dakotah Territory. And not a very treasured part at that. It was peopled "by turbulent and lawless individuals," Governor Faulk told the Dakotah legislature in Yankton that year, and characterized by "a state of society bordering on anarchy."[20]

Then the railroad passed by. The census of 1870 found sixty-nine towns and villages and a population approaching ten thousand, 10 percent of whom, it was noted, worked directly for the UP. And the new settlers wanted their own government. "What may be very wholesome [for] the Norwegians at Yankton," a Cheyenne lawyer declared, "is far from meeting the lightning like necessities of a people whose every movement is made at the rate of twenty-five miles an hour."[21] The editor of the Cheyenne *Daily Leader* agreed. "Dakotah is a slow coach," he wrote. "We travel by steam."[22] And so did Governor Faulk. "In view of the railroad facilities possessed by the territory," he noted, "and the vast beds of coal and precious metals, we may reasonably anticipate for Wyoming a career of prosperity."[23] But if the UP was the making of Wyoming, Wyoming, as soon became clear, more than returned the favor.

As always, prosperity was a drawing card. Even before the railroad passed through, the Blair brothers had company in the coalfields. E. P. Snow and George Young opened mines in the immediate vicinity, and two other entrepreneurs started operations at Evanston, ninety miles west, and at Carbon, one hundred miles east, of Bitter Creek.

In Boston, meanwhile, UP officials were holding a series of meetings with a certain Thomas Wardell, the owner and operator of several successful coal mines in Macon County, Missouri. With no coal department or mining expertise of its own, the railroad decided to let a contract for the development of its coal properties, and that contract had gone to Wardell. By its terms, he would open mining operations at promising points along the line and dig the company's coal for a reasonable profit while the UP would control all subsequent sales and all distribution.

Wardell paused just long enough to incorporate the Wyoming Coal and Mining Company and then sent his brother Charles to the Wyoming hinterlands. Charles opened the company's first mine at Carbon in 1868 and a second one several months later at Point of Rocks. Pushing on, he came across a spectacular outcrop at the eastern edge of the Bitter Creek valley and immediately ordered Point of Rocks closed and the whole camp—processing plant, mine office, section houses—shipped to this new location, which he named Rock Spring (the s was added some years later) after the nearby stage station.

Charles founded one other mine in the Bear River Valley near Evanston and then rested. Thus it was that on the eve of the inauguration of transcontinental rail service in the summer of 1869, the Wardells and the independents squared off against each other across the sagebrush wastes of the three largest coalfields in the West.

Though the battle lasted a full three years, the independents never had a chance. The UP, naturally, used its own coal to fire its trains, so

Thomas Wardell, owner of the Wyoming Coal and Mining Company and one of the founders of Rock Springs. (Photograph from The Sweetwater County Historical Museum, Green River, Wyoming)

the contest was to supply the homes and businesses of Wyoming and Nebraska. The independents struggled mightily to keep down their expenses, to mine coal for less than it was costing Wardell, and they had some success. But in the end it didn't matter, for however cheaply the Blairs or George Young might be able to get their coal out of the ground, they still had to transport it to Laramie, or Cheyenne, or Fort Kearney, and there was only one way to do that—over the rails of the UP. After the independents finished paying ruinous UP freight rates and adding this expense to the price of their product, their coal, on the average, sold for twice as much as that of the railroad. The independents, for example, paid $10 a ton to ship their coal to Omaha—where UP coal sold for $9. In Odgen, to which freight rates were the same, UP coal sold for $6.50.

But the abuses didn't end there. To increase production and cut costs, the UP put in sidetracks to all its mines in early 1870. And the results were predictably dramatic: Production in Rock Springs jumped from six cars a day to twenty-five. At the same time, the vice president of the UP directed the general superintendent "not to allow any side-tracks to be put in at any mine along the line of the road except those of the Wyoming Coal Company."[24] Not surprisingly, Archie and Duncan Blair were reduced in no time to peddling their product locally to those customers who could be reached by wagon, and then, thanks to another directive, only to those who didn't work for the UP.

The independents—and a great majority of the citizens of the High Plains—were outraged: The railroad was supposed to bring prosperity to the West; instead it was bringing ruin. Wyoming's governor sent a sharply worded protest to the secretary of the interior, charging that UP freight rates were "obstructing the development of the country,"[25] and the Cheyenne *Daily Leader* called the company "a curse to the community for its outrageous and discrminating freight and passenger tariffs."[26] Most appalled of all were the railroad's own government directors, three private citizens appointed by the president to sit on the company's board and represent the views of the public at large. They found the situation "an inexcusable iniquity," as they wrote in their report to the president for the year 1872:

> It is difficult to estimate the injury resulting to all legitimate interests from the [Wardell] contract. The country through which the Union Pacific Railroad passes needs cheap fuel. Fuel deposits are unlimited and of easy operation. Fuel ought to be cheap. Active competition in its production will assure this. Reasonable and uniform rates of transportation will, if the coal lands are not held in monopoly, stimulate production and establish competition. This will tend to develop the country along the line of the road, increase the general and local businesses of the line and greatly enhance the probabilities of an ultimate return to the Government of [its] large investments in the road.

> We think the entire policy touching the coal lands and interests of the Union Pacific Railroad Company unfortunate and unwise and we cannot give it our approval. . . . Its existence can in no way be justified. We have tried long and persistently to rid the company of the [Wardell] contract, [but] we have failed to effect this end.[27]

And for good reason. For while the arrangement with the Wyoming Coal and Mining Company may have been ruinous to local communities and the U.S. government, it was a financial windfall for its stockholders. And except for Wardell, who owned 10 percent of the stock, these were none other than half a dozen of the board members of the Union Pacific Railway Company.

One by one, the independents folded. First the Blairs, then George Young, then the Creighton brothers in Carbon—all of them "absorbed" by the Wyoming Coal and Mining Company. A few small operators, such as E.P. Snow, continued to sell coal locally, but otherwise by 1873, Wardell and the UP had a virtual coal monopoly in Wyoming. "Our coal mines have proved fully equal to our most sanguine expectations," UP President Oliver Ames declared, "both in regard to the superior quality of the coal and the extent of the deposit. There is no better coal in this country and none where it can be mined more cheaply."[28]

As the independents fell, production at Carbon, Rock Springs, and Evanston soared, from a combined output of 7,000 tons in 1868 to 50,000 tons a year later, to 200,000 tons in 1875. Lacking any outside competition, the three Wardell camps competed with one another to be number one. Carbon led in the beginning, with twice the output of Rock Springs and nearly three times that of Evanston. But Rock Springs, whose coal was of a higher quality than Carbon's, was gaining steadily; in 1871, Mine Number One came into its own, doubling the camp's output in a single year. And in 1873, Wardell opened a second mine on the Bitter Creek outcrop. The following year, Rock Springs took the lead in production and never lost it thereafter. When Carbon closed for good in 1902, a total of 4.5 million tons had been taken from its mines. Total output from Rock Springs for the same period was more than three times that figure.

Rock Springs not only outperformed Carbon; it outperformed every other coal camp west of the Missouri. By 1875, Mine Number One, "Number One" to anyone in the business, had become the most productive—and most famous—coal mine in the West; Rock Springs alone was now supplying half of all coal used or sold by the UP. In the six years since Charles Wardell closed Point of Rocks and moved it lock, stock, and barrel to the giant outcrop by the banks of Bitter Creek, Rock Springs had become one of the most important coal towns in America.

Aside from coal, and the money to be made from it, Rock Springs had little to recommend it. In a state top-heavy with spectacular

Mine Number One in Rock Springs, the biggest producer west of the Missouri, 1879. (Photograph from The Sweetwater County Historical Museum, Green River, Wyoming)

scenery—the Tetons, Yellowstone, the Wind River Range, Devil's Tower—Wyoming's southwestern corner seems cruelly neglected. Rock Springs lay at the western end of the Red Desert where prairie succumbs to dryness and a pale brown pallor extends for over 150 miles. With the odd sandstone mesa the only relief, the baked alkali and laterite crust stretches over arroyo and ravine from horizon to horizon. The weather is the sun and the wind—sometimes alone, sometimes in tandem—sucking the landscape dry and carrying it off over Nebraska and Iowa. "The snow doesn't melt here," a local saying holds. "It just blows back and forth until it wears out." When the first church was being built in Rock Springs, the wind blew it down three times. "So rapid is the disintegration of the sandstone bluffs," wrote Captain Stansbury, "and so constant the wash of the soil that the valley is almost entirely destitute of even a spear of grass and presents a most desolate appearance."[29]

The soil is so bad in this corner of Wyoming that a grazing cow needs forty acres to survive. The Shoshoni, who should have known, estimated it would take all the natural products of twenty-five square miles of such country to sustain a single brave for one year. "Of what earthly use is this awful country?" a passenger once asked the stationkeeper in Rock Springs. "Well," the gentleman is said to have answered, "it helps hold the two ends of the country together."[30]

Yet the terrain managed a certain austere grandeur from time to time, as even Stansbury was obliged to concede: "The escarpments," he noted, "rounded into fantastic forms of bastions, buttresses, and turrets by the action of the winds and rains, were in many cases quite beautiful."[31] There is, moreover, the constant play of sun and shadow on the reds and yellows of the sandstone and limestone bluffs as the puffy cumulus clouds sail past in the wind.

Before man—and before the Rockies—the region was the floor of a great inland sea. As the sea receded, semitropical forests of elm and maple and magnolia covered the marshy plains, eventually dying out as the water dried up, petrifying, and becoming coal. Later, millenia of volcanic violence covered the old seabed with their residue, only to give way, after eons of wind and sun, to the curious landscapes of today.

Two hundred miles east of Salt Lake, eight hundred west of Omaha, at an elevation of 6,200 feet, Rock Springs sat in a wide bowl between low rolling hills to the south and white limestone cliffs to the north. East and west lay open to the desert and the wind. Bitter Creek, sixty feet across, twelve feet deep, wandered through the middle of the bowl, stagnant or dry most of the year, a roaring wet menace in the spring—"a sluggish, alkali stream, the entire absence of which would be no special loss to the town."[32]

Dominating the valley is a great ridge that sweeps down out of the north and then veers suddenly westward a mile short of the town. Flat and sheer at the top, White Mountain spreads out at its base where centuries of runoff have gouged deep gullies in its flanks. The snow, which never lingers in the bowl at the mountain's feet, gathers in the ravines and suggests winter late into spring (and gives the great bluff its name). The formation stretches for fifteen miles, as far as Green River, a great wall looming over the railroad tracks. To the north lies one of the world's largest bodies of shifting sand, and north of the sand, clearly visible from the top of White Mountain, sit the snowcapped summits of Washakie's beloved Wind River Mountains.

Conditions in the two coal camps at the foot of White Mountain, Rock Springs and Blairtown, were primitive. The earliest inhabitants were almost exclusively male, most of them young bachelors in their twenties or thirties, or family men without their families. Many came from Wardell mines in Missouri, and the rest came from coalfields farther east. In both instances, a good number were either "Lankies," from the coalfields of Lancashire, England, or Scandinavians. Many of the nonmining support jobs—muleskinners, loaders, blacksmiths—were held by ex-railroad workers, generally Irish, or disappointed gold seekers, with the odd fugitive and desperado thrown in. The work was seasonal and most of the workers transients, looking to lay aside some savings and then move on to start, or return to, a family.

They wasted little of their earnings on housing, choosing instead to hole up in dugouts burrowed into the banks of Bitter Creek. Earth-walled on three sides, these dugouts sported crude wooden doors slapped across the fourth side and breathed through a stovepipe poked into a dirt roof. The story is told of an enterprising candidate for the territorial legislature who was out canvasing for votes one day and, not knowing a dugout when he saw one, fell through a dirt roof into the living room of six startled Finns. "The way these six Finns jumped up from their supper and looked at me," the candidate later recalled, "I think if I'd been on a platter I'd 'a been a gone goose."[33] These Bitter Creek caves, as they were known, fine much of the year, were regularly flooded out every March or April. Most of their owners waited patiently for the waters to recede and then dug a new hole. Those who preferred the relative safety of higher ground shivered in makeshift tents.

Some good derived from this annual cleansing, however, as a local poet was moved to observe:

> O Classic Creek! Rich in tradition
> Of tragedy and superstition,
> Your yearless, reckless inundation
> Provides the means of sanitation.
> Besides, the lord knows very well
> When you have purged yourself of smell
> And other things that much displease,
> You've freed the town of foul disease.[34]

"Rock Springs was a desolate, dreary town," an early observer noted, "a collection of shacks and tents. On the barren windswept plains of Wyoming, Rock Springs grew without planning in every direction. Streets seemed to wind at their own inclination and they were alternately dusty, muddy, and frozen."[35]

And it was the frontier besides: Indians hunted on the edge of town, outlaws robbed trains in broad daylight, rustlers roamed the open range, and Butch Cassidy wintered at nearby Brown's Hole. The closest law was a hundred miles away in South Pass. Life in Wyoming in the 1870s and 1880s was "hell on women and horses," one wag observed, and Rock Springs was no exception.[36]

Social life, what there was of it, "was still in swaddling clothes"[37] and centered almost exclusively on the saloon, the "poor man's club," where miners gathered after work to fill their lunch buckets with lukewarm ale ("the cup that cheers"), read the Salt Lake papers (those who could), and try their luck at cards. There were cowboys too: "They might ride through the front door into a saloon, rein their horses at the bar, and order a whisky 'neat' without getting out of the saddle, but no barkeeper ever took issue with them, knowing they had money ... and would spend it for liquor with a lavish hand."[38]

And "working women"—to help the single man pass the long lonely nights.

Butch Cassidy, whose first name came from a stint he spent as a meatcutter in the town, frequented many of these saloons and was once nearly arrested in one:

> Practically everyone in Rock Springs knew that Butch Cassidy made his headquarters in Brown's Hole, but no officer felt the urge to go in after him. . . .
>
> The day came when news reached David G. Thomas [the "Classic Creek" poet], a young officer, that Cassidy was staging a spree in one of the saloons. Thinking to put one over on older minions of the law and claim the large reward being offered, the young deputy armed himself, entered the saloon, and spotted his intended victim. In the hilarious crowd he was unnoticed as he carefully maneuvered his way to a position directly behind his man. Then, thrusting his gun in the outlaw's ribs, he shouted, "Stick'em up!"
>
> Cassidy was taken completely by surprise. Thomas looked determined and seemed to have the weight of argument on his side.
>
> "Looks like you've got me this time," smiled the outlaw. "I ought to be arrested for being so careless. Well, I guess that calls for a drink all around. You don't mind, Sheriff, if we have just one more before I go to jail? It'll probably be a long time before I get another."
>
> "I guess one more won't do any harm," agreed Thomas, trying to be a good sport.
>
> "Belly up to the bar!" shouted Cassidy. "The drinks are on me!"
>
> The bartender filled the glasses. "Here's how!" said the prisoner, and every man lifted his glass, including the young deputy. Just at that moment Cassidy pulled his own gun, catching his captor off

*Miners' dugouts built into the banks of Bitter Creek.
(Photograph from The Sweetwater County Historical
Museum, Green River, Wyoming)*

*Bitter Creek in flood. (Photograph from The Sweetwater
County Historical Museum, Green River, Wyoming)*

guard, disarmed him, and backed out into the night.

"Charge that one to the sheriff!" he called as he vaulted into the saddle.[39]

Brawls were commonplace, often getting out of hand. Witness the demise of Charles Wardell, the brother of Thomas and founder of the camp at Rock Springs. Wardell had words at a dance one night with a certain Bobbie Frew. Frew brought the discussion to a close by pulling a knife and slicing Wardell open the width of his abdomen. Holding his innards in place, Wardell staggered into the coatroom, fished out his pistol, staggered back into the dance hall, and shot Frew through the chest. Bobbie died on the spot; Wardell, a few hours later.

Justice in southwestern Wyoming was in the eye-for-an-eye tradition. Take the case, from Carbon, of Dutch Charlie and Big-Nose George, two notorious train robbers. A pair of popular deputy sheriffs were following the outlaws' trail one day and had just stopped to examine a still-smouldering campfire when they were gunned down by Charlie and George, who had been hiding in ambush. Charlie was captured several months later and sent by train to the county jail in Rawlins. When his train stopped in Carbon to take on coal and water, an angry mob of miners stormed aboard, overpowered Charlie's guards, and dragged the outlaw onto the platform. "Give me a sporting chance," he pleaded as he was hustled down the street. "Don't string me up. Turn me lose and shoot at me." But the mob was having none of it. They tossed a rope over the crossarm of a telegraph pole, stood the ashen-faced Charlie on a barrel, and cheered "as a little Swede kicked the barrel from under him."[40]

Not surprisingly, Rock Springs had an undertaker several years before it had a doctor and a jail long before a city hall. The earliest inhabitants loved to tell how funerals were always being held up while miners ransacked the town to find a woman who could pray.

Services and amenities were few. The hotels were famous for what they lacked: ice water, room service, screens, and bedsprings (though there was no lack of bedbugs—or drafts in the winter). Mail was flung on a large table in the boxcar-cum-post office, and residents helped themselves. Ed Clegg hauled water from a spring north of town to storage barrels in front of houses or to board-lined cisterns where it was dipped with old powder kegs. Mountain fever was rampant. "Rock Springs was like a dozen other mining towns you could name, neither better nor worse. A pitifully small number . . . of spiritually-minded men and women did their best to combat the rude temptations of the town, while the open saloon continued to compete with the gambling den for the dollars the mothers of little children needed for food and clothing, and 'up on the hill' the noise of a rickety piano joined with the obscenity of fallen women."[41]

One of the first ladies of quality in town was Mrs. Archibald Blair, whom Archie married in Canada and brought to Rock Springs in 1870. She found the town an acquired taste: "She was used to a life of culture and order in her Canadian home, but she met the changes in civilization cheerfully and courageously."[42]

It was "an unattactive little town," an early Wyoming senator summed up his impressions of the place, "set down in what was practically a desert, beside a stream of unsavory reputation, whose waters furnished no refreshment to man or beast. One is tempted to wonder if any good could ever come out of such a place."[43]

After 1871, Rock Springs began to grow up. In that year, Mine Number One first "came in as a substantial producer, and on the output and quality of Number One the village rode into place."[44] In just four years, the population of the camp tripled, from four hundred to twelve hundred, and the community slowly shed what an early detractor called its "air of jaunty impermanence."[45] In 1870, there were three frame houses in the entire camp; three years later, there were two streets of nothing but wooden houses, and the first store had opened (owned and operated by one Molasses Johnson, so called because of his near-exclusive diet of molasses and crackers). Before long, there was a butcher shop, a barber shop, a harness maker, a tailor, even a boot- and shoemaker, and merchants and tradesmen now stood at the bar with cowboys and lived across the street from coal miners.

Meanwhile, workers were putting the finishing touches on the most impressive and most significant structure yet erected in southwestern Wyoming: the two-story stone headquarters of Thomas Wardell's Wyoming Coal and Mining Company, which was now moved from Missouri to Rock Spring. This edifice, deliberately located some distance across the tracks from the camp, housed the company store and post office on the ground floor and company offices on the second. The Wardell Building, as it was known, exuded confidence in the camp's future and soon inspired a spate of further construction. Two new hotels sprang up, the American House and the Railroad House, the latter, according to a letter in a Cheyenne paper, "one of the cosiest little hotels—[with one of] the finest billiard rooms—on the line of the UP."[46] Wardell, meanwhile, threw up even more housing, mainly for company officials. Called pepperboxes after their shape, these new structures were either built on the spot or constructed in Omaha and shipped to the scene. In both cases, to Wardell's great satisfaction, they were "strong enough to have served as forts."[47]

There were women and children in Rock Springs now, as railroad officials and coal-company managers moved in with their wives and merchandise stores (themselves an innovation) made room on their shelves for parasols and hoop skirts, copybooks and wooden toys. On weekends, a man now had to choose between the horse races and pigeon shoots at the edge of town or going to the calico-and-overall dances where the ladies were wont to waltz with glasses of water on their heads. Or they might prefer the basket dances where each lady brought a picnic basket that went to the highest bidder at lunchtime, which gentleman thereby bought the right to partner the lady in the afternoon. There were married miners now too, and soon there would be a school, a church, and a band. As one pioneer cattleman noted, "Barbed wire and women are the two greatest civilizing agents in the world."[48]

All the excitement and prosperity was confined to the Wardell camp; at the opposite end of the valley, dwarfed by the output of Number One and crippled by ruinous UP freight rates, Blairtown was dying. After the Wardell Building went up, residents of Rock Springs demanded that the railroad station and post office, two boxcars beside the tracks, be moved to their end of the valley. By 1873, the UP had moved both facilities, and most of Blairtown—some fifty souls or so— soon followed. Archie and Duncan sold out to Wardell, and their camp, the first of its kind in Wyoming, was eventually absorbed by its ever-expanding neighbor to the east, whose residents, to mark their community's dawning respectability, now took to adding an *s* to its name and thereafter called it Rock Springs.

Between 1871 and 1875, as Number One made a town out of Rock Springs, coal production and profits shot up fourfold. While the UP was certainly grateful for the good news, the company in the beginning did not pay any more attention to its coal department than to its other operations. By 1875, however, all that changed as the company reeled from a series of staggering reverses that raised havoc with passenger and freight revenues, sent UP stock into a dangerous tailspin, and brought the young railroad to the brink of bankruptcy.

The first blow came in the fall of 1869, only five months after through service to the Pacific was inaugurated, with the opening of the Suez Canal. Shipping revenues dropped steadily as the lucrative

China trade from the East Coast and western Europe was lured off the freight cars of the transcontinental railroad and on the clipper ships and packets of a new generation of shipping companies. "The road to India," as Grenville Dodge had styled it, no longer lay across America.

The advent of the steamship was still another setback for the company. Steam more than halved travel time by boat from New York to San Francisco or the Orient. The railroad was still the fastest way across the country, but boats were cheaper and much preferred by the shipper who wasn't in a hurry. Moreover, East Coast companies trading with the Orient, who would have to transfer rail-shipped goods to boats in San Francisco in any case, preferred to ship all the way by sea. Expensive rate wars erupted as the UP and other lines slashed freight rates to compete with the steamship companies.

Another blow came from the citizens of Wyoming via the U.S. Supreme Court. The railroad always maintained that as it had been chartered by Congress as a public service, it should be exempt from the state property taxes all other businesses were obliged to pay. Since the UP was by far the largest company in Wyoming, this exemption rankled. In 1873, the territorial legislature in Cheyenne passed an act canceling the company's special status. UP lawyers fought the legislation all the way to the Supreme Court—and lost. Thereafter, one-third of Wyoming's total property-tax revenue came from the UP.

That same year also saw the start of the depression that became known as the Panic of 1873. "Like a black dividing line," one historian has written, "the Panic cuts across the history of the 13 years following the Civil War. On the one side lies the sunshine of buoyant commercial prosperity; on the other the gloom of depression and poverty."[49]

The Panic, more severe than the Great Depression of the 1930s, was in large part the result of the overbuilding and overcapitalizing of railroads, both in the United States and on the Continent. Banks failed, industry reeled, unemployment soared. The UP suffered along with everyone else; shipping and passengers revenues dried up, coal prices plummeted, building came to a halt.

As the company absorbed these and other shocks, including a demand from the government to start paying at least the interest on the huge loan it had received from the U.S. Treasury, rumors began to spread about the railroad's solvency. A suit filed in Cheyenne in May 1870 brought the matter into the open. James Davis, a construction contractor, claimed the company owed him $600,000 for services rendered. The presiding judge, John Howe, ordered the railroad to put up the disputed amount in security while the case wound its way

The railroad depot. (Photograph from The Sweetwater County Historical Museum, Green River, Wyoming)

through the courts. When UP attorneys offered as security a bond signed by several company directors, Howe stunned the courtroom by refusing to accept it, proposing instead to place the assets of the road in the hands of a receiver. The UP, in Judge Howe's mind at least, couldn't be counted on to cover its debts.

UP President Ames called the action "an outrage" and ordered immediate retaliation. "If this is submitted to," he wrote Dodge, "any thief or swindler that swears the Company owes him anything can have a receiver appointed and charge a commission on the value of the road."[50] Ames didn't say so, but his biggest concern was that the company's books in all likelihood could never have withstood the close scrutiny of a receiver.

The unlucky Judge Howe soon learned, in the words of a UP spokesman, that "there is a very short and swift retribution for men who deviate from the paths of rectitude." Railroad attorneys "descended on Cheyenne, the Justice Department outlined to other Wyoming judges the government's desire to see the road kept running, and Howe found his own removal imminent."[51]

Within two weeks, Howe backed down, and the case proceeded without a receiver. Ames pronounced himself "gratified that the

Wyoming courts have come to their senses."[52]

Alarmed by this close call, the company took a number of steps to curb falling profits and otherwise protect its interests in the territory. On the latter note, Ames decided the railroad should involve itself more directly in local politics and had funds set aside for use during the congressional election of 1870. Wyoming's man in Washington should be a strong supporter of the railroad, Ames declared, and he dashed off a letter to Republican officials in the territory to offer the UP's services in the upcoming contest, "provided the Republicans will nominate a man selected by the officers of the Railroad."[53] The man the company had in mind was one Church Howe (no relation to the judge in the Davis case), but Governor Campbell and much of the Republican party in Wyoming considered Howe a buffoon and eminently unelectable. As if to prove the point, the boorish Howe traveled the territory giving out free UP passes and boasting that his election had "all been fixed in Boston" (UP headquarters). In due course, Ames relented and threw his support behind the party's man, who went on to win the election. General Dodge, in a letter to headquarters, drew the moral of the tale. "It is necessary," he wrote, "for us sometimes to interfere in matters where we have great interests at stake, but it should be done in such a manner that our action should never be known."[54]

But whatever the company might do to protect its flank, the real problem was still the same—falling profits. By 1875, only land sales and coal revenues kept the company afloat, the latter in particular. At all three mining locations in Wyoming, production was stepped up. New seams were developed as fast as they could be discovered, and in Rock Springs two new mines, complete with their own camps, were opened. In less than six years, the company's coal mines had evolved from one of several sources of revenue to the key to the company's continued success. "Those mines," Governor Thayer wrote, "are absolutely necessary to the comfort of the people living along the line of the UP Railroad, and to the railroad itself to enable it to carry on its operations."[55] Charles Adams, a later president of the railroad, was more direct: "Those mines," he declared, "were the salvation of the Union Pacific."[56]

Thus it was that the much-maligned coal camp by the banks of Bitter Creek, now the source of half of all UP coal, suddenly found itself at the center of the mighty railroad's struggle to survive.

3

Perfect Order and Peace

Does your union propose to dictate to this company regarding the amount of coal it is to mine? [For] if that is your purpose, gentlemen, I herewith give you notice that in a very short time I will have a body of men here who will dig for us all the coal we want.

—S. H. H. CLARK,
General Superintendent, Union Pacific

I n early March of 1874, Jay Gould became the controlling stockholder and chairman of the board of the Union Pacific, and a new era dawned in the coalfields of southwestern Wyoming. One of Gould's first acts was to commission a review of all the company's major departments, and he was astonished to discover that coal production, the most crucial area of company operations, was being managed by an outside contractor. After less than two weeks in office, Gould ordered the termination of the Wardell contract, the creation of the Union Pacific Coal Department, and the forcible seizure of all company mines.

There were several reasons behind Gould's actions, but the most important was money. According to Gould's arithmetic, in the six years since Thomas Wardell incorporated his Wyoming Coal and Mining Company and began selling coal to the Union Pacific at a profit averaging $4 a ton, the contractor had netted himself a tidy $2 million. With Wardell out of the way, these profits could go directly into the railroad's coffers, and the railroad, the Lord knew, could certainly use them. What's more, beyond Wardell's legal profits, Gould smelled some illegal ones. "I have had a conversation with Mr. Gould," one high company executive wrote to a colleague, "in reference to Wyoming coal matters and he thinks it very important now that Mr. Wardell be brought to account for the money received by him while an officer of the Wyoming Company. We are satisfied that he has 3–500,000 dollars to account for and we want the money back."[1]

There was also the matter of the curious composition of the board of directors of the Wyoming Coal and Mining Company, most of whom were also major stockholders and high officials of the Union Pacific. These gentlemen benefited handsomely from the arrangement, pocketing profits once from coals sales and then again through any increase in the price of company stocks and through yearly dividends they were paid (in direct violation of congressional legislation). Gould was concerned about the double-dipping and conflict of interest involved, and he was also concerned about being left out.

Wardell got wind of the impending takeover and hurried to Boston to try to stop it. On March 17, while Wardell was away, a Mr. Musgrave and a Mr. Clark walked into the headquarters of the Wyoming Coal and Mining Company in Rock Springs and handed a letter to superintendent William Mellor. The two men represented something called the Union Pacific Coal Company, the letter explained, and they had orders to take possession of the building and the surrounding mines. Mr. Wardell would be compensated in due course.

Mellor refused to comply and promptly cabled Wardell for instructions. "Give up possession under protest" came the answer from Boston, and Mellor obeyed. That same day, railroad representatives also seized the mines at Carbon and Almy, outside Evanston. Wardell sued to stop the action and was eventually awarded a $100,000 settlement, but he never got his coal mines back. Shortly after the takeover, he moved back to Missouri and was never seen in Rock Springs again.

It was all in a day's work for Jay Gould, the "Wizard of Wall Street" and entrepreneur par excellence, one of the most successful— and most feared—businessmen of the last half of the nineteenth century. Gould, a "certifiable crook" and millionaire by age twenty-two, came to prominence just as the power of capital in America, as yet unchecked by government legislation or the presence of organized labor, was at its zenith. In that twilight era, wealth was power, and as one of the three or four richest men of his time, Gould was automatically one of the most influential. One biographer wrote,

> None of his contemporaries quite approached his genius for trickery, his boldness in corruption, his talent for strategic betrayal, his mastery over stock and bond rigging, his daring in looting a company

and defrauding its stockholders. Daniel Drew warned that his touch was death, and James Keene, another ex-collaborator . . . declared him "the worst man on earth since the beginning of the Christian era." His skill at dealing and trading was so notorious that even the sophisticated financiers of Europe feared to join in any of his schemes. Once on a brief visit to the continent he sent in his calling card to one of the Rothschilds. It was returned with the scrawled comment: "Europe is not for sale."[2]

The flamboyant Gould had his hand in virtually every major business undertaking of the day; the Pacific Mail Steamship Company, one of the largest shipping outfits in the country, was a Gould enterprise, as were Western Union and the New York *World*. And he also owned nine railroads, with a total of 14,043 miles of track, more than ten percent of all railroad mileage in the United States. "One man holds almost undisputed sway over the movements of the Stock Exchange," a contemporary journalist wrote of him. "No such example of one-man power has ever been known in Wall Street. Under these extraordinary circumstances, to write of the New York Stock Market is simply to describe the movements of Jay Gould."[3]

At his death in 1892, Gould "was worth approximately 100 million dollars, which he acquired along with the title of the most hated man in America."[4]

Jay Gould.

Determined to stem the tide of corporate red ink (and add to his own fortunes), Gould ordered a wage cut for all company miners. Thanks to the Panic, explained D. O. Clark, manager of the Coal Department in Rock Springs, the price of coal was falling all across the country, and the price of mining it would have to fall as well. A similar wage cut in the East had precipitated a serious miners' strike, but the colliers in Wyoming had no union. They protested the action and then grudgingly submitted. In the months that followed, the men in Carbon and Rock Springs were organized into local chapters of the Miners National Association.

The following year, in the summer of 1875, as coal prices continued to fall, Gould ordered another wage cut, and this time the men in Rock Springs went out. S. H. H. Clark, general superintendent of the UP, based at field headquarters in Omaha, hurried to the scene to negotiate. The miners wanted wages restored to five cents a bushel, the rate before the cut. Clark offered them four. They agreed, provided the company store reduced its prices on foodstuffs and mining supplies. Clark accepted the terms, and the strike was called off.

The settlement lasted three months and then fell apart. Without any warning or explanation, prices were suddenly raised again at the company store. When the miners complained, the company ignored them.

The Rock Springs chapter of the Miners National Association met twice a month. At the second meeting in October, the membership voted to call a strike for November 8 unless the UP raised wages back to five cents a bushel, and, to show they meant business, the miners also voted to begin working only half days as of November 2. The next night, miners in Carbon passed identical resolutions, and on November 3, union men at the Excelsior Mining Company in Rock Springs, an independent operation, made the same five-cents demand of company president E. P. Snow. Meanwhile, the slowdown had begun as scheduled the day before.

Gould welcomed the action. He had watched the spread of unionism in the coalfields with growing alarm. Because of the UP's near-complete dependency on coal to run its trains and to stay solvent, and because of the unique situation whereby one town supplied over half the company's needs, the railroad was especially vulnerable to labor agitation. A single well-timed strike—in Rock Springs, in the winter—could easily cripple the company. A union, in short, could not be allowed in Wyoming, and Gould was anxious to make that point, to confront and in the process destroy the Miners National

Association before it won any more converts. Gould ordered Clark back to Rock Springs to make whatever arrangements were necessary to keep the company's mines open. Clark was forbidden, however, to make any concessions to the would-be strikers or to take any other steps that might legitimize their organization.

The confrontation between unions and the railroads, between labor and capital, of which the trouble in Wyoming was but the latest episode, had been brewing for several decades since the rise of industrialization and the subsequent appearance in the American workplace of that curious new phenomenon known as the wage earner—the man who, for a fee, did another man's work. As the inevitable abuses of this employer-employee dynamic became more numerous and widespread, wage earners sought solace and strength in numbers, and various fraternal and trade associations sprang up in the 1840s and 1850s. Largely social in nature in the beginning, these brotherhoods became more militant after the Civil War as mechanization grew more rampant and capital became increasingly concentrated in the hands of powerful corporations—when the wage earner, in short, came to realize that his status as a worker was in all likelihood permanent and that his relation to his employer, as a consequence, would henceforth be adversarial.

By the early 1870s, organized labor felt sufficiently powerful in certain professions to confront these corporations and demand certain rights and conditions for the workingman. Not surprisingly, the nation's railroads, among the largest of these corporations—the key to the success of many of the country's industries and the central symbol of economic growth and progress—were at the heart of this struggle.

Among the most victimized and militant of America's wage earners were colliers, and one of the first great clashes between unions and the railroads took place in the Pennsylvania coalfields in December 1874 when members of the Mine and Mine Laborers Benevolent Association struck the mines of the Philadelphia and Reading Railroad, demanding a 20 percent wage increase. The Philadephia and Reading, supported and encouraged by the rest of the railroad fraternity, refused the demand, and the strike dragged on into the new year. By February, the walkout was becoming a hardship for many miners and their families, but it was kept alive by threats from the notorious "Molly Maguires," a secret highly influential ring of violence-prone extremists dedicated to freeing the collier from the tyranny of the railroads and their stalking horses, the coal companies. By March, having identified the real enemy, Franklin Bowen, president of the Philadelphia and Reading, contracted with the Pinkerton Detective Agency to infiltrate the Maguires' high command, and a certain James McParlan, posing as a fugitive from justice, was sent into the coalfields and subsequently recruited by the sect.

Playing his part to perfection, McParlan won the order's trust and in time became the friend and confidant of its leadership, whom he then exposed to state and federal authorities. Twenty-four of the order's senior operatives were later tried for murder, arson, theft, and destruction of government property, and fourteen were eventually hung.

Meanwhile, the Long Strike, as it was called, ground on through the spring and finally unraveled in June when impoverished colliers, abandoning their union in droves, returned unconditionally to the mines. And promptly had their wages cut. The debacle, especially the connection with the Molly Maguires, proved the undoing of the Miners and Mine Laborers Benevolent Association, and within a year the organization had collapsed.

Unionism was right where Jay Gould wanted it, on the run, and he seized the opportunity to finish in the West the job the Philadelphia and Reading had begun in the East. He passed on the wage cut that had been ordered in Pennsylvania to his own mines in Wyoming, thus precipitating the strike in June, eventually culminating in the crisis that now loomed in Rock Springs.

General Superintendent Clark, who had negotiated the earlier settlement, hurried to the scene from Omaha. Clark was a courteous soft-spoken man with a reputation for patience and fairness, and was highly regarded by miners and company officials alike. He arrived in Rock Springs on the morning of the fifth, three days before the strike deadline, and met with union leaders in the afternoon. Wages could not be raised, he told the miners, and the company would expect the customary 25 percent winter production increase during the next three months. For its part, the UP promised to fire Thomas Musgrave, manager of the company store, and guarantee the previously agreed-upon price cuts. He then added, "in a firm but gentlemanly manner," that he did not believe the men could find higher wages anywhere, but if they wanted to try, he would provide them with railroad passes. Union leaders said they would put Clark's offer to a vote by the full membership and give him their answer that evening.

Governor Thayer was also in Rock Springs that day, the first time a governor had visited the town, and he was asked to appear before a miners' meeting. The overflow crowd rose politely as the governor entered, and listened respectfully to his remarks. He urged the colliers not to strike, promising that he would take whatever steps necessary to keep the mines open, and warned them against any violence or damage to company property. The men "pledged themselves to his Excellency to keep the peace and not to interfere with the property of the coal companies" and then rose again as the governor left the hall.[5]

That evening, Clark and the governor returned to union headquarters to receive the miners' decision on the company's offer. It was no: The colliers would not work for less than five cents a bushel, and they would not dig the customary 25 percent winter supplement. Clark lost his habitual self-control upon hearing the news and delivered a sharp rebuke to the union leaders, which was reprinted in local papers the following day: "Does your union propose to dictate to this company regarding the amount of coal it is to mine? Do you intend to limit our supply of coal from our own mines? Do you wish to cripple us in failing to give us an adequate supply of coal for the purpose of running our trains and to supply the needs of the people residing along the line of our road? If that is your purpose, gentlemen, I herewith give you notice that in a very short time I will have a body of men here who will dig for us all the coal we want."[6]

There was little doubt about the composition of this "body of men" Clark spoke of; they would be Chinese laborers recruited from San Francisco. The Chinese were Gould's ultimate weapon, the reason he had never doubted who would win in any confrontation with coal miners in Wyoming. They were known to be quick studies, tireless workers easily managed, and, most importantly, they refused to join labor unions. Worked by the Chinese, the Rock Springs coalfield would always be open, which, given that field's prodigious output, meant that a strike against the company by miners at any other camp could never hope to succeed; as long as Rock Springs was open, a strike could never work, and as long as Rock Springs was mined by the Chinese, it always *would* be open. Under the circumstances, a miner's union would have very little to offer the average collier.

But that wasn't all: Guaranteeing an uninterrupted supply of coal from Rock Springs not only struck a mortal blow at unionism inside the UP but could also enable other railroads to neutralize the threat from organized labor, for the supply of coal from Rock Springs was enough to permit the UP to sell coal to other lines in the event of a strike against them. Rock Springs coal, the lifeblood of the UP, could, in

Governor Thayer. (Photograph from Wyoming State Archives, Museums and Historical Department, Cheyenne)

transfusion, become the lifeblood of other railroads as well.

Superintendent Clark and Governor Thayer left Rock Springs the morning after their meeting with union leaders. Before his departure, Clark left instructions with company officials to contact a certain Mr. Beckwith in Evanston to begin negotiations for procuring a Chinese work force for Rock Springs and Carbon.

Mr. Beckwith was quite willing to help the UP, but his terms were stiff: In return for his services, which would include recruiting and then managing a Chinese work force for Rock Springs and possibly Carbon, the railroad must pay all transportation costs associated with the contract; must agree to make Beckwith the sole provisioner of all the labor he hired and the sole payroll agent for all UP miners–whether hired by him or not; and must sell to him its merchandise stores in Almy, Carbon, and Rock Springs, which stores were the chief competition to similar establishments operated by Beckwith's Beckwith, Quinn, and Company at each locale. But the UP agreed to the terms, and Beckwith contacted his agents in San Francisco.

On November 6, two days before the strike deadline, E. P. Snow at the Excelsior Mine told his workers they could dig coal for four cents a bushel or they could quit. They quit. Snow, who had been stockpiling coal against just such an eventuality, paid off the strikers on the spot and promised them that when his mine reopened in the spring, they would be standing in line to work for three cents a bushel. On the seventh there were rumors that strikers were planning to take over the company store and seize UP mines.

On November 8, close to 500 miners at Rock Springs and Carbon walked off the job, closing down the two largest coalfields of the UP system. At the same time, the Miners National Association sent notices asking other chapters in the region to honor the strike and not to dig any coal destined for use by the UP.

The mood turned nasty. Company officials, on order from Omaha, immediately fired the strikers and paid them off. The union countered by throwing up pickets at all mine entrances, coal chutes, and power plants. Hardliners threatened to set fire to the mines and other company property, including locomotives. A shot was fired at mine superintendent Tisdale. The UP called on Governor Thayer for protection.

The governor ordered one company of U.S. soldiers each to Carbon and Rock Springs on the twelfth and then proceeded to the scene himself. The troops arrived in the middle of the night and quietly took up positions in front of all mine entries, coal sheds, engine houses, and other buildings belonging to the railroad. The startled strikers woke up on the morning of the thirteenth to an armed camp: " 'Murther alive! What's this now?' was the exclamation of Tom Kinney as he stepped out onto the platform this morning to get a breath of fresh air. 'Holy Jesus, boys, if here ain't the sogers!' And sure enough there before our astonished gaze were the bluecoats, their bayonets glittering in the frosty air and their measured tread falling strangely upon the quiet town."[7]

The strikers demanded an audience with the governor. The meeting was brief and much less cordial than a week earlier. The miners called for the immediate withdrawal of the troops, but the governor refused, promising that the troops would stay where they were as long as there was any threat to UP property or the welfare of the people who were in need of the company's coal. He urged the miners to call off their strike and return to work or face the consequences. Clark, who had come that day from Omaha, was also on hand and hinted again of replacing the strikers with Chinese. After he and the governor left, the miners held a general meeting and voted to continue the walkout.

As the strike entered its second week, many colliers began to grow restless. Family men watched their money and food supplies dwindle, and rumors about the impending arrival of a trainload of Chinese "scabs" were becoming more persistent. "The mines will probably be in full blast within the next ten days," the strikers read in the Laramie *Daily Sentinel* on the morning of the thirteenth, "but what will be the complexion or nationality of their occupants [this reporter] sayeth not."[8] Miners who talked of leaving to look for work elsewhere were threatened and warned not to break ranks. A gloom settled over the town. "A great deal of drinking is going on," wrote another reporter, "more than I have ever witnessed in this place before."[9] On the eighteenth, the tenth day of the walkout, the union called meetings in Carbon and Rock Springs to review the situation; by small majorities, both chapters voted to continue the strike.

Three days later two UP trains left Sacramento for Rock Springs, carrying 150 Chinese laborers. Railroad officials notified Governor Thayer of the trains' expected arrival time and advised him to send two more companies of troops to the coalfields. Thayer wired General Crook in Omaha and took an overnight train to Rock Springs.

Once again, the troops arrived at night, followed later in the forenoon by the governor, Clark, and A. C. Beckwith. The three men conferred through lunch and then left at 2:00 P.M. in Clark's private car, heading west. A heavy wet snow began to fall, blanketing the ground in a matter of minutes.

At 4:15 P.M., the governor and his party returned, escorting the two trainloads of Chinese strikebreakers. As the miners looked on, "some in grim silence, some with their native Irish wit and humor, and others with wailing and gnashing of teeth,"[10] the trains pulled up near Mine Number Three, and the Chinese piled out. Some fell to work at once, making cooking fires, while others unloaded a string of boxcars laden with lumber and other building materials. The Chinese ate hurriedly and spent the night in boxcars.

The next day, a Chinese camp rose out of the snow-covered ground near Mine Number Three, a quarter mile north of the center of town. All day, company carpenters pounded small wooden cabins together, and tracklayers built a spur to the new camp. Armed soldiers were everywhere. Once again, the colliers asked to see the governor: "Governor Thayer met the miners this morning and in his remarks gave them distinctly to understand that legitimate labor should not be interfered with, no matter what the nationality of the laborer might be, and that law and order would be enforced if it took the entire U.S. army to do it."[11]

Later in the day, a brief notice appeared on the wall outside the company store:

All persons whose names appear below can obtain employment in Mine No. One. None others need apply.
All miners desiring passes for themselves and families east or west must apply at once, as none will be granted after November 24.[12]

Two-thirds of the fired strikers looked in vain for their names. They had just over two days to get out of town.

On the morning of the twenty-third, a five-man committee appointed by the union asked for a meeting with Clark to plead for a settlement. If the Chinese left, the committee promised, all miners would return to work at prestrike wages. Clark spurned the offer. "The next 24 hours," observed the *Daily Sentinel* correspondent in his dispatch that evening, "will probably witness the departure of many, if not the majority, of the residents of this once quiet and prosperous burgh."[13]

The following morning, November 24, was the last day strikers and their families could travel free on the railroad. The 10:00 A.M. eastbound train was jammed with angry miners. Not far from Rock Springs, the colliers stormed into first class, kicked out its startled occupants, and rode the rest of the way to Omaha in style.

Back in the town, 50 whites and 150 Chinese reported for work in the mines. The names of the whites were checked off a list before the men were allowed to descend. Several men not on the list also reported but were refused entry. Throughout the day, company officials observed operations:

The Chinese have commenced their labor and are running out the coal in as good a condition as in days gone by. They are delighted with the prospect before them and the company are perfectly satisfied with the result of the first day's labor. The Excelsior Coal Company today notified all miners that had been previously employed by them that they could obtain passes until tomorrow at 6:00 P.M. by calling upon Mr. Snow. This move on their part would seem to indicate that they too do not propose to trade any longer with strikers. ... Much as this step is to be regretted by all interested in the welfare of our young Territory, it may be and probably is the only way to a successful solution of this vexed question at the present time; but we do sincerely hope and anxiously look forward to the day when capital and labor shall find its equilibrium and the Caucasian race be the only laborers employed throughout our borders.[14]

Jay Gould was glad to have his coalfields back, and he directed UP President Dillon to convey his appreciation to Superintendent Clark and Governor Thayer. "We feel well satisfied with the way you have handled the strike in the mines," Dillon wrote Clark. "Hold a tight leash on them now."[15]

And the governor was happy too: "The property of the coal company has been protected," he wrote in a special message to the territorial legislature, "and the mines are now being worked with satisfactory results. Perfect order and peace have been maintained."[16]

4

Arms and Belly Muscles of Steel

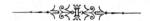

*The strike is over at Rock Springs, but the effects will be seen in
Wyoming long after the circumstances have faded from our
memories.*

—LARAMIE *DAILY SUN*
NOVEMBER 26, 1875

One hundred and fifty Chinese reported for work at Union
Pacific coal mines in Rock Springs on the morning of November
25, 1875. U.S. troops escorted the sojourners to and from the
pits and stood guard at each entry, but there were no incidents, and the
following day the soldiers were withdrawn. By the end of the year,
there were some two hundred Chinese working in Rock Springs and
a year later, over four hundred. Out on the prairie east of town,
company carpenters were busy putting up a small city, promptly
dubbed Hong Kong, to house the daily influx of new laborers. White
miners who had not been dismissed stood quietly by and watched.
"The strike is over in Rock Springs," the Laramie *Daily Sun* editorialized,

but what a change! In place of the ambitious and progressive coal
miner—a thinking being with whom we could converse and who
was proud of his American citizenship—what have we now? A rice
eating Chinaman! A being that is brought to this country about the
same as foreign cattle and horses are, [and] imported and hired out
by their employers in pretty much the same manner. They work
cheap; they don't strike; they ain't particular about their quarters;
they don't put on airs; don't know when they are swindled, and
don't even want as much land as will make a ___ hole in the ground.
...The evil we feared would result from the action of a few hot-headed
miners at Rock Springs has come upon us, and now we must all

suffer the consequences.

Yet it is our candid opinion that the Union Pacific managers never made a greater mistake than when they employed these same Celestials.[1]

Perhaps, but Jay Gould didn't think so. After all, if the strategy worked and kept organized labor out of the coalfields, it could mean great profits for the UP. On the other hand, the company had to tread more lightly than Gould would have liked. While the company could in theory hire whomever it pleased, in practice the Union Pacific dared not exclude white labor altogether from Rock Springs. There was, alas, public opinion to think about. The railroad was at least in part a public corporation; over $26 million of its construction costs had been paid, via a government loan, by the U.S. taxpayer, and even now three government directors appointed by the president sat on the board and watched out for the public's interests and its investment. Under the circumstances, it was not politic for the company categorically to deny work to white coal miners, especially if, as the UP insisted, they were willing to sign the notorious "ironclad," an agreement wherein the wage earner promised never to join a union, on pain of immediate dismissal.

But if the company couldn't keep the white man out as a matter of policy, it could keep his numbers (hence his influence) minimal, chiefly by making working conditions so unpleasant that few white men would apply. And so it happened that within a year of the coming of the Chinese, A. C. Beckwith and Coal Department officials devised and implemented a series of policies so draconian and blatantly discriminatory that the average white collier was loath to work for the railroad or if he was hired, soon found conditions intolerable. "When Beckwith Quinn became the lessees of the coal mines," a local labor leader noted some years later, "then truly was the iron hand and glove bared to oppress and degrade white labor. . . . Labor with them possessed no rights. The wants of women and children meant nothing. . . . The Chinese Kings would just as soon employ monkeys . . . if thereby they could appropriate all the proceeds of labor."[2]

Even then, thanks largely to the ravages of the depression that now gripped the country after the Panic of 1873, many of the miners still living in Rock Springs—as well as those who came from the East in search of work—found the company's terms, distasteful and humiliating as they were, preferable to not working at all: "They were compelled by the force of circumstances . . . to work under such dishonorable and oppressive conditions. . . . Many a miner had paid out his last dollar to railroad companies on account of transportation for himself and family, and had a hungry wife and starving children demanding to be fed by his labor."[3]

The UP could hardly have found a better choice for labor boss in the coalfields than A. C. Beckwith. A kind of frontier Jay Gould, he was an enormously shrewd and successful businessman and no friend of the wage earner. He first went to Wyoming as a young man to trap in the Rockies and numbered Jim Bridger and Kit Carson among his boon companions. He switched from trapping to trading and opened a store at Fort Phil Kearney where he was on hand to help bury the eighty soldiers killed in the Fetterman massacre. The next season, he was in Cheyenne, running the first store in the city. "All the worst men on earth have come here," he wrote his family. "All kinds of crimes you can imagine are committed and most of them unpunished by law. To live here a man must be made of cast iron."[4] He would have written sooner, he went on to explain, but his pride prevented him from writing until he was prospering.

He crossed the territory just ahead of the UP and settled for a time in Echo, Utah, where he bought out a general-merchandise business. The business flourished, and he opened branches at other locations in Utah and in Wyoming, in Evanston, Rock Springs, and Carbon. In 1872, he moved to Evanston and bought a ten-thousand-acre cattle ranch. In only nine years, his business had grown from the small wooden store in front of Fort Phil Kearney into a chain of general-merchandise outlets with an annual profit of nearly $1 million.

To Beckwith, the Rock Springs Chinatown was just another business, to be run as all his other ventures were—to make the greatest profit. Under the circumstances, the more Chinese he hired, the more money he made.

To appreciate the impact of the measures Beckwith et al. introduced into Rock Springs, it is necessary to understand how coal was mined in the West in the late 1800s and to know something of the life of a collier. On a typical day, the coal miner rose before dawn, pulled on his pit clothes, ate a hurried breakfast, and made for the mine while the rest of Rock Springs slept. He lived either in his own small frame house, usually rented from the company, or, if he was single, in a cramped boardinghouse where he shared a room with three or four other men and took his meals. With him he carried his tools and lunch

A mine entry. (Photograph from The Sweetwater County Historical Museum, Green River, Wyoming)

Inside a room. (Photograph from The Sweetwater County Historical Museum, Green River, Wyoming)

bucket, and on his head he wore an oil lamp. Each morning, the prairie east of town swarmed with the flickering lights of scores of miners picking their way, like so many fireflies, through the blackness to work.

He carried a crushing collection of tools: one 18- to 20-pound drill, eight or nine 3-pound picks, a 6-pound sledge hammer, a shovel, a scooper, tamping needles, a steel wedge, and a keg of gunpowder. Some of these he stored in a shed near the mine entrance, and the rest he hauled back and forth from his lodgings.

When he arrived at the mine, he tossed his tools into a "pit car," jumped in, and rode this "man trip" (as opposed to a coal trip) down the "entry" to the vicinity of his "room." An entry was the ten feet wide by six feet high track-lined main street into the bowels of the mine, the thoroughfare by which miners came and went and out of which teams of mules dragged brimming pit cars. Rooms were hot, stuffy affairs, located up narrow corridors off the entry or one of its branches. A typical room was twenty-four feet wide, several feet deep, and not quite high enough for a man to stand up straight.

Just getting to his room from where the pit car left him, often half a mile or more away, down cramped passageways likewise too low for a man to stand erect, was an exhausting business. "Before I had been down a mine," George Orwell noted fifty years later in writing about similar collieries in England,

> I had vaguely imagined the miner stepping out of the [pit car] and getting to work on a ledge of coal a few yards away. I had not realized that before he even gets to work he may have to creep through passages as long as from London Bridge to Oxford Circus. . . .
>
> At the start to walk stooping is rather a joke, but it is a joke that soon wears off. . . . You have not only to bend double, you have also got to keep your head up all the while so as to see the beams and girders and dodge them when they come. You have, therefore, a constant crick in your neck, but this is nothing to the pain in your knees and thighs. After a mile it becomes (I am not exaggerating) an unbearable agony. . . . You try walking head down as the miners do, and then you bang your backbone. . . . This is the reason why in very hot mines, where it is necessary to go about half-naked most of the miners have what they call "buttons down the back"—that is, a permanent scab on each vertabrae.
>
> But what I want to emphasize is this. Here is this frightful business of crawling to and fro, which to any normal person is a hard day's work in itself; and it is not part of the miner's work at all, it is merely an extra. The miner does that journey to and fro, and

sandwiched in between there are seven and a half hours of savage work.[5]

As soon as he arrived at his room, the collier set to work. Hunched over, naked except for boots, kneepads, and a pair of light drawers, the collier grasped a pick in one hand, a sledge hammer in the other, pressed the pick against the edge of the seam, and struck over and over, moving the pick along the perimeter of the coal until a black chunk splintered off and dropped at his feet. "Coal," Orwell wrote, "lies in thin seams between enormous layers of rock so that the process of getting it out is like scooping the central layer from a Neapolitan ice."[6]

When he tired of pick-and-hammer work, he took up his shovel and began loading the coal wagon, which stood outside the room, just beneath the level of the door. "It is a dreadful job," Orwell wrote of this shoveling,

> an almost superhuman job by the standards of an ordinary person. For they are not only shifting monstrous quantities of coal, they are also doing it in a position which doubles or trebles the work. They have got to remain kneeling all the while—they could hardly rise from their knees without hitting the ceiling. . . . Shovelling is comparatively easy when you are standing up, because you can use your knee and thigh to drive the shovel along; kneeling down, the whole of the strain is thrown upon your arm and belly muscles.[7]

All the while the miner was obliged to see to his oil lamp, a cumbersome device in which oil burned through a wick, forcing the collier to lay down his tools every so often, locate his iron lamp pick, and raise the wicking. The lamps gave off nearly as much smoke as light, quickly fouling the air in the cramped rooms.

From time to time, to widen a seam or uncover a new one, the collier would set a charge in the rock. "Before they could blast any coal loose, they had to first cut a gash or 'kerf' about five feet deep under one wall of the room. To do this a miner lay on his side in the thick carpet of coal dust covering the floor [and] swung his pick at floor level to cut the gash. As he pulled out the coal his pick knocked loose, he was nearly buried in slack. Then he cut a vertical gash either at one corner or through the center of the face."[8]

Next the miner opened a 15- to 30-inch-deep hole in the wall with his breast augur, cleaned the hole with his scraper, and inserted a cartridge filled with gunpowder. To insulate the explosion and confine its impact inside the wall, he stuffed tamping all around the cartridge, then carefully pulled a needle out of the center of the charge and inserted a squib or fuse into the groove. When all was ready, he lit the fuse, yelled "Fire!" and scrambled for cover.

Miners worked in pairs, and a man prayed for a good partner and a good room, in that order. A collier was as loath to work with a poor partner, the saying went, "as he would have been to marry a girl who could not cook." The first question of any partner was always the same: "Buddy, how are you with a pick?" The handling of a pick "was looked upon as nearly comparable in precision to that of handling a billiard cue."[9] Many men preferred to work with their sons, who were sometimes no more than nine or ten years old.

Once the coal wagon outside the entrance to the room was full, a driver, or sometimes the miners themselves, guided it carefully along the corridor to the entry. This manuever was fraught with risk, especially in those places where the grade was steep, for the ropes and poles needed to restrain the brimming car often broke, sending the loaded wagon crashing out of control down through the passageway and out into the open mine. In some mines, chutes were installed in the rooms; all the miner had to do was shovel his coal into the chute, and it tumbled out a minute or so later in the entry. This was the case in some of the lower workings of Number One and was an arrangement much favored by miners as it increased their production, hence their earnings.

Once a trip or train of loaded cars was assembled in the entry, teams of mules dragged it up the rails to the mine entrance, often a distance of a quarter or even a half mile, up angles as steep as thirty-five degrees. Outside, the coal was either loaded into other wagons and driven to the railroad tracks or, after spur lines were built, hauled directly in the pit cars to trackside chutes where screeners picked out the slack (the finest screenings) and shoveled the rest down the chute into waiting coal cars. In time, huge slack heaps built up and became common features of the landscape.

Screeners were one of many support occupations necessary for the operation of a large mine. Others included pit bosses, one inside and one outside each major entry; their boss, the mine superintendent; and the man above him, the general manager. And bosses, as well, for the blacksmith shop and the stables. And woodcutters, mule drivers, water carriers, loaders, unloaders, wheelwrights, coopers, carpenters, blacksmiths, stable hands, and payroll clerks—a complete contingent for each mine.

*Digging coal. The miner lying on the ground is digging a
"kerf." (Photograph from The Sweetwater County
Historical Museum, Green River, Wyoming)*

In winter, the season of peak demand, the collier worked a 10- to
12-hour day, starting as early as three or four in the morning, during
all those hours coming above ground only once, for the midday meal.
He rode up in a pit car and sat outside enjoying the fresh air and the
company of his fellow miners. After a heavy lunch of rabbit (or elk or
beef), potatoes, biscuits, and canned corn or tomatoes, he descended
for several more hours with the pick and shovel. To save time and
make more money, some miners skipped the trip to the surface and ate
sitting on gob piles down in their rooms.

On a good day, a man could dig and load nine tons, roughly one
ton every hour. After the slack, for which he was not paid, was
screened out, his output came to nearly six tons, which, at seventy
cents a ton, made a daily wage of $4.20. Compared to the cowboy or
sheepherder (who made $1.00 a day) or the tailor or shoemaker (who
made $3.00), it was a decent living, on a par, for example, with that of
a railroad conductor. A miner's tools came out of his salary, however,

reducing it by as much as 20 percent, and there was also the fact that the work was seasonal; the miner who worked ten hours a day in January might work only three or four in July, and some days not at all. Many colliers left Rock Springs altogether during late spring and summer, causing an annual dip in the population. Others worked out a lucrative summer strategy whereby they spent the requisite hours each day digging what coal the company needed, and then, instead of going home when the whistle blew, they stayed on and dug coal for themselves. They stockpiled this excess coal in their rooms until winter came and demand was up, when they sold it in addition to their daily tonnage. Some miners stored as much as four or five hundred tons in their rooms. "Several men who were later to become affluent citizens of Wyoming laid the foundations of their fortune in this manner."[10]

The collier's day ended around three or four in the afternoon

Mules hauled coal and men out of the mines. (Photograph from The Sweetwater County Historical Museum, Green River, Wyoming)

Loaded cars and slack heap at Number One. Mine Superintendent Tisdel is at extreme right. (Photograph from The Sweetwater County Historical Museum, Green River, Wyoming)

when he carried his tools to the entry and caught a man trip up into the daylight. Once out of the mine, the first thing he did was to gargle a small amount of water to clear the coal dust from his throat. "When the miner comes up from the pit," Orwell wrote, "his face is so pale that it is noticeable even through the mask of coal dust. This is due to the foul air he has been breathing and will wear off presently. To [someone] new to the mining district, the spectre of a shift of several hundred miners streaming out of the pit is strange and slightly sinister. Their exhausted faces, with the grime clinging in all the hollows, have a fierce, wild look."[11]

The collier went home after work, usually via his favorite saloon, read his paper or smoked his pipe, and kept an ear cocked for the mine whistles. Every evening, after the day's production was tallied up and measured against orders, these whistles, each in a different register, blew the signal for "work" or "no work" on the morrow. The mine at Central went first, in its "rich baritone," followed by the "fine tenor" in Blairtown, and the contralto of Lady Megeath. But the climax was the mighty bass of the Union Pacific at Number One:

> Great is the stir as he gallantly takes the stage . . .
> Many men in his employ and he must please them.
> So pours forth his melodious notes,
> Thundering back and forth in echoes,
> That all must report in the morning
> And fill the Union Pacific orders.
> The miner at rest in his little home
> Lowers his paper to inform his wife
> That he wants ham in his bucket instead of beef.[12]

It was brutal, hellish work by any standards—"exaggeratedly awful," Orwell called it—executed under appalling conditions half a mile beneath the surface of the earth. Often as not, the collier rose and went home in the dark, sometimes not seeing sunlight for days at a time. Hour after hour he stood hunched over in his hot, stuffy room, breathing its poisoned air, a perilous mixture of oxygen and coal dust, all well mixed with the noxious fumes of his oil lamp and his gunpowder, while that same dust made a black mask of his face, caked his nose and ears, and clogged the pores of his skin. "The place is like hell," Orwell declared, "or at any rate like my own mental picture of hell. Most of the things one imagines in hell are there—heat, noise, confusion, darkness, foul air, and, above all, unbearably cramped space. Everything except the fire, for there is no fire down there except the feeble beams of Davy lamps . . . which scarcely penetrate the clouds of coal dust."[13]

And it was astonishingly dangerous work, the most dangerous in the world. Mine accidents took a myriad forms: runaway pit cars, collapsing rooms or entries, falling rock, flooding, suffocation, cave-ins after explosions, and, most feared and lethal of all, underground gas leaks. As they chipped away at the walls around them, miners routinely opened fissures in the rock face, releasing invisible, odorless gases. The gas then seeped unseen into rooms and out into corridors and entries, growing more and more volatile under the pressure of cramped quarters until it either exploded spontaneously or was ignited by sparks or a miner's oil lamp. Wherever a leak was suspected, a pit boss rushed to the scene and let loose a canary. If the canary died, the men had only a few minutes to get out before the explosion. In 1881, thirty-five Chinese perished in such an explosion in Almy. For years, the number of accidents per tons of coal mined climbed steadily.

Had the mining of coal somehow taken place in the public eye, one suspects society would have outlawed it.

Small wonder, then, that the collier was sensitive about his wage. You could not, after all, properly compensate a man for the daylight he never saw, the clean air he never breathed, and for risking his life daily. His salary was not so much a compensation as a bribe.

Who was this collier? What kind of man would do such a job? Very few miners chose their profession; most simply inherited it as a kind of dubious birthright. They were born into mining families in mining communities in coal country where for generation after generation, the people had known no other trade, no other world. The work also held a certain perverse appeal to masculine pride, the status of belonging to that courageous elite who practiced the world's deadliest craft. And the risks, moreover, created a powerful bond between colliers; a miner would do anything for his partner or for the other men in his entry, the men who dug you out of the rubble of a collapsed entry or pushed you out of the path of a runaway pit car. Theirs was a world unto itself, but it offered its inhabitants the security and identity of any tightly knit brotherhood.

Whoever he was, however he came by his profession, whatever the reasons that drove him to enter the mines day after day, society, Orwell observed, owed the coal miner a staggering debt:

> Practically everything we do, from eating an ice to crossing the Atlantic, and from baking a loaf to writing a novel, involves the use of coal. For all the arts of peace, coal is needed; if war breaks out, it is needed all the more. . . . It is April but I still need a fire. Once a fortnight the coal cart drives up to the door and men in leather jerkins carry the coal indoors in stout sacks smelling of tar and shoot it clanking into the coal-hole under the stairs. It is only very rarely, when I make a definite mental effort, that I connect this coal with that far-off labor in the mines. It is just 'coal.'
>
> It is so of all types of manual work; it keeps us alive and we are oblivious of its existence. More than anyone else, perhaps, the miner can stand as the type of the manual worker, not only because his work is so exaggeratedly awful, but because it is so vitally necessary and yet so remote from our experience, so invisible, as it were, that we are capable of forgetting it as we are capable of forgetting the blood in our veins. All of us really owe the comparative decency of our lives to the poor drudges underground, blackened to the eyes, with their throats full of coal dust, driving their shovels forward with arms and belly muscles of steel.[14]

These were the men the UP now set out to humiliate. The first hurdle to becoming a UP miner was the ironclad, an agreement every collier had to sign, wherein he promised, on pain of dismissal and the loss of one month's pay, not to join a labor union. Even then, the company consistently gave hiring preference to Mormon miners over other whites, for Mormons did not join unions.

But getting a job was only the beginning; a collier's real problems started after he was hired. The Chinese were routinely given the most productive rooms and were always allowed first choice of rooms when a new entry was opened. Whites, on the other hand, were assigned to the least desirable rooms—the most dangerous, for example—or the most poorly ventilated or (the most common complaint) rooms where they were obliged to cut through great quantities of rock to get at the coal and to which they might have to spend hours laying track. And even then, when they had such a room in working order, they were often forced to turn it over to a sojourner and go to work someplace else. "I was compelled to work an entry in which there were three feet of rock," one miner testified. "After driving through the rock I was compelled to give up the entry to a Chinaman, who had refused to work it while the rock remained an encumbrance."[15]

"I have been driven from two places to make room for Chinamen," another miner related. "I have had my cars checked by them, and upon applying to the boss for redress was told that if I did not like it, I could take out my tools."[16]

Whites were required to have a permit before working in a given room, but not the Chinese. In many entries where whites worked, man trips were eliminated, obliging the miner to waste valuable time walking to and from his room, carrying fifty pounds or more of tools. Whenever an entry was closed, the Chinese were assigned at once to a new one, but not the whites: "Myself and son worked in No. Five Mine. The mine was closed down by the company in the early spring. At the time of its abandonment there were employed in it about equal numbers of Chinese and white miners. The Chinese were given employment in other mines without delay, while the white men, including myself and son, were refused employment, without any alleged reason or cause, for the space of two months."[17]

There were other abuses:

We have been engaged driving entry in No. One mine and have been compelled to remove from six to fifteen inches of rock for which we received no compensation, although work of this character is considered extra. We were also compelled to drive break-throughs (airways) for nothing; the boss telling us that in case we refused, Chinamen would do it. We were compelled to lay our own track, with short rails, afterwards replacing them with long ones, thus making double labor for us without any additional pay. We presented our grievance to Mr. D. O. Clark, who promised redress, referring us to Superintendent Brown; and upon our applying to the latter gentleman he stated that he could do nothing for us, that he (Clark) had made us no such promises.[18]

There was also harassment from the Chinese, who were not above taking advantage of their privileged position. They stole the white collier's pit cars, ripped up his tracks, baited him with insults (a reprisal could cost a man his job), and even on occasion stole his coal: "Any white miner resenting such a theft was, upon the yell of the contesting Mongolians, instantly surrounded by 100 picks and drills furiously brandished by 100 excited, jabbering Orientals. Of course the white man went to the wall on every occasion. A white man striking a Chinaman was discharged immediately, while a hundred Chinamen charging one white man with picks and drills to take his life was a subject for much fun and laughter in the office of the company."[19]

There was discrimination outside the mine as well, most of it involving practices at the Beckwith Quinn store. (Quinn was a partner whom Beckwith eventually bought out.) Chinese bought their tools at cost, but whites paid the retail price. During a certain period, miners hired through Beckwith were forced to sign an agreement that obliged them to trade at his store exclusively and allowed Beckwith, as a consequence, to raise his prices with impunity. Flour and sugar, for example, cost twice as much as at competing stores. Any collier who made purchases elsewhere and was found out was fired or had the amount of these "illegal" purchases taken out of his salary, which was funneled through Beckwith since he was the company's payroll agent. Many miners never saw any cash at all; their entire earnings were owed to the store long before payday came around.

And there was no redress. Any collier who complained about conditions risked losing a month's pay and being reassigned to a bad room; in fact, he was required to sign a paper agreeing to these penalties: "As soon as we would [complain] the next thing we heard was a telephone message to mine No. so and so to discharge that man.

I remember last fall when eight others went to the office here to present a part of their grievances to Mr. Tisdel [and] he would not hear their complaints because they had signed this agreement or contract."[20] "He was asked to be dumb upon the question of his wrongs," wrote the former president of the miners' union local. "He was refused the right of petition, the right of meeting with his fellows for the purpose of remedying his wrongs, or even discussing them. He was asked to sign away his free speech, his liberty and his manhood."[21]

Nor was there any possibility that conditions might change any time soon. The local chapter of the Miners National Association lay in shambles, and within a year persistent strikes and the arrest and trial of its founder had destroyed the union nationally as well. Beckwith's terms, such as they were, were not going to get any better; the white miner could take them or leave them. Many took them.

In the end, the company hired more whites than it planned on, generally maintaining a white-to-Chinese ratio of 1 to 3 or 1 to 4, but never hired enough to jeopardize operations. The work force was expanded considerably during the period following the strike, as the company opened three new mines in Rock Springs and overall coal production tripled, from 104,000 tons in 1875 to 306,000 in 1884, with Rock Springs consistently accounting for half the combined output of all company mines. The main beneficiaries of this expansion were the Chinese, whose numbers increased from 200 in 1875 to 400 in 1876, to 600 by the end of the decade. (Most, but not all, of these Chinese worked in mining; a small percentage worked on section gangs in charge of maintaining and repairing track, and made Rock Springs their headquarters.) The number of white colliers rose from 50 in 1875 to 150 ten years later.

To house the immigrants, a new city rose up out of the sagebrush and greasewood wastes just east of Mine Number Three. As was the case wherever the sojourner went, he lived apart, constructing his own closed community, a complete society unto itself, and as exact a replica of a typical Cantonese village as could be managed on the edge of the Red Desert. For the sojourner, after all, was the most reluctant of immigrants; deep in his heart, he had never wanted to leave the Celestial Kingdom, in the first place, and in Chinatown, the idea was, he need never feel that he had. For all the contact between Chinatown and white town, just a mile up the tracks, the Chinese might have lived on a different planet. And for all the whites actually knew about them, they might have come from one.

Chinatown sat at the base of the eastern edge of the great rock

butte that towered over Rock Springs to the north, on the opposite side
of the tracks and the river from white town. At its peak, Hong Kong
had over 650 residents and over eighty houses. Half the houses were
sturdy wooden structures built by the company and rented to the

*The Company Store. (Photograph from The Sweetwater
County Historical Museum, Green River, Wyoming)*

Chinese, and half were makeshift shacks thrown together with packing crates and building paper, their roofs made from flattened tin cans. As a rule, company employees, 80 percent of the camp, lived in company housing when there was enough, and others—merchants and tradesmen—put up their own accommodations. In addition to homes, there was a sprinkling of other buildings, including restaurants, an occasional boarding house, herb shops, laundries, a Joss House (temple), and the clan headquarters.

It was an all-male world, two-thirds of the men unmarried, almost all under the age of thirty-five. They lived five and six to a cabin, more in the cold months, and took their meals out, in noodle shops or at the clan headquarters. Most, like their white counterparts, were either pick-and-shovel men or in support positions, such as mule drivers, woodcutters, loaders, unloaders, blacksmiths or water carriers. A few were bosses. The only women, less than ten, were the wives of these supervisors, plus a handful of prostitutes.

At the heart of the social order in the Chinatowns of the West was the clan. The basic social unit in the Celestial Kingdom was the extended family or clan, which often included everyone in a given area with the same surname. An entire village or district might contain no more than three or four such surnames. The good—and the good name—of the clan came before the interests and concerns of the individual, and in turn the clan looked after its members and provided for their comfort and security. Smaller clans from the same district or speaking a common dialect often joined together into clan associations. During the period of Chinese immigration, the largest of these associations maintained representatives in San Francisco, and most immigrants were either recruited through or managed by these agents. Later, these associations evolved into the famous Six Companies. Thus the sojourner who settled in Rock Springs was secured through his association on the West Coast and came in with others of his clan. A community the size of the Rock Springs Chinatown probably contained members of no more than two or three clans.

The social center of every large Chinatown was the clan headquarters. From here the clan arranged for and managed nearly every aspect of the sojourner's life. Here was his bank and his post office, his meeting hall, banquet hall, and funeral parlor. It was here that he came to gamble and from here that his bones could be shipped back to China for burial. Ignorant and suspicious of the American legal system (and effectively excluded from it), the sojourner turned to the clan for the resolution of disputes and the dispensing of justice.

Ah Say, patriarch of the Rock Springs Chinatown, with his wife. (Photograph from The Sweetwater County Historical Museum, Green River, Wyoming)

Ah Koon, with his famous fur coat. (Photograph from The Sweetwater County Historical Museum, Green River, Wyoming)

The clan even arranged, by proxy, that most important of all annual rituals, the visit to the graves of one's ancestors.

For these services and others clan members paid annual dues. While in some respects the clan association was all-powerful and autocratic, in most cases the sojourner submitted willingly to its control; unmarried, cut off from his family and culture, he craved the security and sense of belonging the clan provided—the proof, in short, that he was still Chinese.

At the top of the clan hierarchy and social structure in Hong Kong sat Ah Say, the undisputed leader of the Chinese community. Ah Say had lived in America since 1857 when he came to work in the California goldfields. Later he became a labor contractor for the Central Pacific. When the transcontinental was completed, he moved to Evanston and took up his trade there, supplying several local mining companies with Chinese workers. At the time of the strike in Rock Springs, his friend A. C. Beckwith engaged Ah Say to recruit labor. Thus, together with his assistant Ah Koon—a dandy remembered chiefly for the long fur coat he wore wherever he went—Ah Say became the manager and chief handler of nearly all the Chinese in Wyoming.

The daughter of a UP official in Laramie remembered meeting Ah Say:

> Ah Say was often in our house in consultation with my father. He was a gentleman, intelligent and most interesting and spoke very good English. He was always bringing us presents of Chinese fruit and nuts and very often more costly and rare gifts. He came one day looking very happy and said he was soon to be married and wanted us to see his wife sometime. He told me rather quietly that she was a little-footed woman. I suppose he did not want to boast too proudly of his great fortune, so he told only me about it.[22]

Ah Say moved to Rock Springs in the late 1870s. A kindly, benevolent old man, he was known for his solicitude toward the needy and the sick. Every Chinese New Year, all the citizens of Chinatown assembled in a large square in front of Ah Say's house to receive the greetings and good wishes of their patriarch.

The sojourner's day varied little from that of his white counterpart. He rose before dawn, drank tea with his cabin mates, ate a bowl of rice or noodles, and went off to the mines. If he was a pick-and-shovel man, he wore a miner's pit clothes, but if he worked above ground, he preferred his traditional Chinese clothes; a loose blue cotton blouse, matching broad trousers, wooden shoes, a jade bracelet, and a broad-brimmed hat made of split bamboo or black felt. Most still wore the queue.

On his way to work, he saw Hong Kong waking up—restaurants and noodle shops serving their morning clients; fruit and meat sellers laying out their wares; fish sellers dropping live fish into tiny artificial ponds; peddlers shouldering immense baskets of vegetables; the attendant sweeping out the temple; ducks, geese, and pigs feeding on the refuse in the gutters.

At lunchtime the sojourner left the mine and came back to Chinatown to his favorite noodle shop or restaurant. Here the fare, straight from the real Hong Kong via San Francisco, was varied and wondrous: chicken, pork, and Chinese bacon; oysters, cuttlefish, and abalone (all dried); seaweed, mushrooms, salted cabbage, dried bamboo shoots, bean sprouts, vermicelli, dried fruits and vegetables; peanut oil, sweet rice, crackers, almond cakes, and tea. After lunch the sojourner napped, then returned to the mine.

In the evening, the sojourner drank, grew loud, and threw his famous self-control to the wind, betting large sums at the mah-jongg or fan-tan tables, sometimes losing a month's wage in a single night. Or he bought the favors of a big-footed girl from Canton.

Or—the strangest apotheosis of all—the stoic penny-pinching Chinaman of the white man's imagination descends a narrow flight of stairs into a low smoke-filled room with an earthen floor and walls of rough board where burning tapers floated in oil and men recline on low mat-covered platforms and rest their heads on blocks of wood. Here he opens a small tin, removes a lump of opium the size of a housefly, stuffs it into the bowl of a two-foot-long pipe, lights it with a taper, lies back, "swallows a cloud and puffs out fog." The habit costs him $1.50 a day, nearly half his salary.

If he got sick, the sojourner went to the herb doctor, who took his twelve pulses, one for each major organ, and prescribed an herbal cure. The patient got the prescription filled at the closet-size herb shop where the herbalist searched through his more than a hundred tiny drawers to find the proper ingredients, which the Chinese then took home, boiled in a pot, and drank. For a shave, he went to the barber, who shaved his entire face, even inside his nose and ears. On New Year's Day, everyone shaved his head.

On Saturday the sojourner went to the temple, or Joss House. There was a small temple in Rock Springs and a much larger one in the

Chinese community at Evanston. Two large painted idols guarded the carved wooden doors. Inside, bright banners and richly embroidered draperies hung from the ceiling and walls, jade and porcelain figurines peered out from behind glass cases, and rows of polished bronze statues lined the shelves. Behind gates of carved teakwood and heavy clouds of scented smoke from burning sticks of joss (incense)—bowls of chicken, pork, rice, tea, and wine at their feet, their faces lit by burning tapers and perfumed candles—sat the raised images of Kwan-Yin and Kwan-Kung, the goddess of mercy and the god of war.

Such gods, the worshiper believed, protected him from misfortune, and he made regular visits to curry their favor. He lay his offerings at their feet, poured wine before the altar, lit candles and joss sticks, and burned spirit papers. The god was also an oracle, and on occasion the worshiper came to ask for advice or a question about his future. The attendant handed him a bamboo cylinder filled with numbered sticks that he shook until a stick fell. The attendant then retrieved the fallen stick, noted the number, found the like-numbered passage in the *Book of Sacred Revelations*, read it aloud, and interpreted the oracle's decree.

The life of the sojourner was grim and unrelieved, and even his pleasures—gambling, drinking, opium—were attempts to escape and forget rather than to enjoy. The only exceptions to this harsh routine were the three or four Chinese festivals celebrated each year in every major American Chinatown: the Ching Ming, or grave-sweeping festival; the Moon festival at rice-harvesting time; the Dragon Boat festival to honor the river gods; and, the largest and most important of all, the festival of the New Year, which, by tradition, was also everyone's birthday.

Though it fell in February, preparations for the New Year festival began months ahead. There were special cakes and decorations to be ordered from San Francisco, delicacies to be baked and put away in large crocks. As the day neared, the normally frugal Chinese took two weeks off from work to clean and paint their houses and storefronts, and have themselves fitted for new clothes. The evening before, they hung oil lamps from their doorways and gathered at restaurants to await the stroke of midnight, announced all over town by the explosions of firecrackers to frighten off evil spirits who might bring bad luck in the new year.

The highlight of the holiday was the dragon parade on New Year's morning. The dragon was a hundred feet long and took forty men to carry. It was made of brocaded silk interwoven with gold thread and had been bought by Ah Say in China for $3,000. "The head

A Chinese miner on his way to work, carrying his lunch bucket. (Photograph from The Sweetwater County Historical Museum, Green River, Wyoming)

An herb shop in Chinatown. (Photograph from The Sweetwater County Historical Museum, Green River, Wyoming)

Ceremonies at the Joss House, probably Evanston.
(Photograph from The Sweetwater County Historical
Museum, Green River, Wyoming)

was like that of a long-horned Texas steer, the mouth was that of a mad
bull, with tongue pronged like a viper. Its eyes were red and green,
bulging out."[23] The dragon carriers assembled at the edge of town and
then brought the beast prancing and dancing into Hong Kong,
threading its way like a giant snake through the narrow streets and
alleys, stopping and bowing in front of each house and place of
business. "It is easy," recalled one old-timer,

> for those of us who were here at that time to visualize Ah Say
> marching at the head of the parade, walking cane in hand, dressed
> in a brand new suit of American clothes, followed by his people
> carrying large firecrackers strung on poles. Then came the "teaser"
> carrying a bamboo pole on which were two multi-colored squares,
> which were revolved immediately in front of the dragon to irritate it

and make it more ferocious in the work of destroying the devils or evil spirits supposed to infest the town. Then followed a large number of men arrayed in ancient Chinese costume and carrying battle axes, spears, swords, and other implements of Chinese warfare. . . . Men beating gongs, exploding bombs, and firecrackers were scattered throughout the process, and the din and racket [were] at times deafening.[24]

In the afternoon, it was time to visit the Joss House in Evanston—meeting friends and clan members there. The UP provided free transportation on this occasion, putting on a special fleet of luxury coaches usually reserved for dignitaries. All of Rock Springs turned out to watch the procession, as tom-toms played and a reed band piped the gaily dressed revelers out of Hong Kong, down the tracks, over the railroad bridge, and into the waiting train. The Chinese waved Chinese and American flags, and colliers' sons set off strings of firecrackers all along the route.

The image lingers. A passerby, a stranger to the scene, would have remarked the festive coming together of two communities and two cultures, a mutual acceptance symbolized by the Americans turning out to cheer on the Chinese and the Chinese waving their tiny paper copies of Old Glory. But the image lingers because it is so unusual; New Year's was virtually the only occasion when Rock Springs and Hong Kong acknowledged each other's existence, and it was essentially a one-way acknowledgment at that (the whites of the Chinese). For the rest of the year, though they worked side by side eight hours a day, five days a week, the American and the Oriental met each morning and parted each evening total strangers, deeply ignorant of the other's way of life. The sojourner rarely ventured into white town, and the white miner almost never entered Hong Kong. Neither spoke the other's language, knew the other's name, or, in the end, recognized the other's humanity. To the white collier the sojourner was a complete mystery, the denizen of an utterly alien world. And vice versa. The two communities sat side by side—and worlds apart.

This mutual ignorance suited both sides well enough. For the sojourner, whose goal was to spend as little time in America as possible, there was no reason to know the American or his culture. Indeed, there was the risk that the more he came to know and understand the white miner, the more sympathetic he might become, and this would not suit the UP, which, as it happened, encouraged and abetted the sojourner's isolation.

Even then, though they often pretended otherwise, many of the

Chinese in Rock Springs knew the meaning of their presence. "Several times we had been approached by the white men," one sojourner later observed,

> and requested to join them in asking the company for an increase in the wages for all, both Chinese and white men. We inquired of them what we should do if the company refused to grant an increase. They answered that if the company would not increase our wages, we should all strike, then the company would be obliged to increase our wages. To this we dissented, wherefore we excited their animosity against us.
>
> During the past two years there has been in existence in "Whitemen's Town," Rock Springs an organization composed of white miners whose object was to bring about the expulsion of all Chinese from the Territory. To them or to their object we have paid no attention.[25]

As for the white man, he stood to gain little by coming to understand the sojourner, for the Chinese was merely a pawn; the miners' real quarrel was with the company. There was not even much hostility toward the sojourner, in part because he was only a tool, but also, more ominously, because the Chinese was in many ways not quite a real person in the white man's mind, not altogether human— at least not in the way the white man was—and hardly worth thinking about.

The effect of Chinatown on Rock Springs was devastating; the town that had boomed before the strike was struggling to survive less than a year later. Many merchants went out of business, and those that didn't fought mightily against Beckwith Quinn's near stranglehold on the miners' trade. A representative of a Laramie bank was sent to Rock Springs during this period to look into the feasibility of opening a branch there, but he was not encouraged: "Its physical aspect was uninviting, its business houses few, and all outward inducements lacking."[26] He agreed with an earlier assessment by one of his colleagues that "Chinamen are too numerous and white men too few."[27]

Deep frustration was the prevailing mood; increased gambling, drinking, and fighting the most common reactions. Transience, after a steep decline in the mid-1870s, was on the rise again. A small corps of company officials and their wives provided a certain veneer of gentility, but there were few other traces of refinement and very little sense of civic pride. Rock Springs, which had briefly been a town, now became a coal camp again. "The Union Pacific is responsible for this,"

Chinese New Year procession in Rock Springs. Note the American flag. (Photographs from The Sweetwater County Historical Museum, Green River, Wyoming)

wrote a Cheyenne journalist. "Rock Springs, with its grand coal mines, should be a city of six to ten thousand inhabitants; it is a miserable Chinatown of twelve hundred population."[28]

There was concern for the future of the territory too: "People Wyoming with Chinamen," noted a Laramie editor, "and it will become a great State—when? Put Chinamen in the coal mines, on the railroad, in the hash-houses, and then watch the development of the country if—you are a Methuselah. . . . The effects of a strike paralyse trade and industry for the moment, but Chinese labor paralyses them continuously."[29]

At its annual convention in 1876, one year after the strike, the Wyoming Republican party, a bastion of UP support, passed a strong anti-Chinese resolution. "The introduction of Chinese labor into this country," it read in part, "is fraught with serious and dangerous consequences."[30] And a series of Wyoming governors, most of them Republican, concurred. "The Chinese do not assimilate with our

people," one declared, "and therefore are not to be regarded as a desireable element in our civilization."[31]

But no one seriously expected the company to listen, for in the 1870s and 1880s, Wyoming and Nebraska were essentially fiefdoms of the UP, and the company was virtually a government unto itself. Jay Gould did as he pleased, and at the moment his pleasure was to transform Rock Springs into a piece of Old Cathay.

5

It Has to Be Done

He say, "What's the matter at Rock Springs?"
I say, "Lots trouble, drive China boys out."
—BROMLEY, *Chinese Massacre*

For nine years the coalfields of the West were quiet. In the conflict between organized labor and the Union Pacific for control of the mining camps, Jay Gould and company had won a decisive victory. Then, in the fall of 1884, seemingly out of nowhere, a new union called two successful strikes on behalf of UP shopmen, and in the ensuing excitement a group of colliers at company mines in Colorado asked to be organized under the new order's banner. For the first time since the strike in Rock Springs in 1875, a union was active once again in the coal camps of the Rockies, and the UP's ten-year dominance of the labor question was about to face organized, serious opposition. Suddenly, the tension that had been building up for a decade in Rock Springs was on the verge of exploding.

The first of the two strikes occurred in early May when the company ordered a 10–25 percent wage cut for all shopmen in Denver. On the fourth, the shopmen, who did not yet belong to any labor organization, took the suggestion of a union leader and went out on strike. The next day, the strike spread to all shopmen on the UP system. The astonished company maneuvered for four days to breach the workers' solidarity and then rescinded the cut. Within thirty days, the Knights of Labor, as the new order was known, had organized railroad workers at every major point on the line.

The strike caught the UP at a particularly awkward moment, in the middle of a leadership crisis triggered by the abrupt conclusion of Jay Gould's tumultuous ten-year stewardship. Though Gould himself had made a staggering $20 million profit on his UP stock, his largely self-serving management had brought the company to the brink of bankruptcy. Expensive rate wars, feverish branch-line construction, and competition from steamship companies—including the Pacific Mail Steamship Company, Jay Gould, principal stockholder—ate heavily into the railroad's profits.

The U.S. government, still waiting to collect the first penny on its $27-million loan, followed the declining fortunes of the company with growing alarm. By law the railroad was required to set aside 5 percent of its annual earnings toward repayment of this loan, but the obligation was consistently postponed. In 1878, Congress increased the figure to 25 percent, still without result. Jay Gould, meanwhile, in open defiance of another clause in the original agreement with the government, continued to pay himself and other major stockholders regular dividends on their investments. By 1884, as interest on the loan was about to surpass the principal, Congress ran out of patience and demanded a yearly payment of 55 percent of the company's profits.

When the news became public, UP stock plummeted to record lows, and the company faced the possibility of imminent foreclosure. Gould turned to Charles Adams, one of the railroad's government directors and a well-connected figure in Washington, to use his influence to save the company. Congress agreed to postpone debt repayments yet again, provided Jay Gould resigned. Gould, anxious to get out now in any case, stepped down, and Adams became the new president of the Union Pacific.

The change in management came in June, some three weeks after the first shopmen's strike. For two months, Adams was busy attending to the company's financial woes, but by August, he was free to take on the labor question. He had been disturbed by the outcome of the earlier strike and was anxious to show labor who was in charge. Accordingly, on August 11, against the advice of the railroad's general manager in Omaha (whom Adams, in a major procedural change, had recently given full responsibility for day-to-day operations), Adams ordered a wage cut for machinists in Ellis, Kansas, and the dismissal of the twenty shopmen who had started the strike in Denver. It was a brazen and tactless move, transparently deliberate union baiting, but Adams thought it was necessary: "This simmering discontent," he cabled General Manager Clark in reference to labor troubles, "is worse than open rupture. . . . I do not believe in the defensive. My inclination is to go out and meet these men and give the thing my own direction. I should therefore force an issue, bringing on a strike."[1]

The day after Adams ordered the wage cuts and the firings, all UP shopmen walked off the job, and two days after that, a union delegation arrived in General Manager Clark's office in Omaha to present its demands. The delegation was headed by Joseph Buchanan, the thirty-three-year-old chief organizer for the Knights of Labor in the Rockies. The tall, slender Buchanan was an engaging, forceful man who, in spite of his youth, had already spent six years in the labor movement and earned a reputation for honesty and firmness. The Knights, Buchanan explained, had four demands: the restoration of wages, the reinstatement of the fired shopmen, that all strikers be allowed to return to work without prejudice, and an end to company discrimination against members of a union (the elimination of the ironclad).

Clark forwarded the demands to Adams, who took a surprisingly conciliatory tone. He agreed to three of the four demands—he was not opposed in principle to the existence of unions—but he insisted that the fired shopmen, the troublemakers from Denver, not be reinstated. But Buchanan wouldn't budge.

The next day, Adams wired he was willing to reinstate all but five or six of the worst offenders from Denver; in particular, he would not reinstate the secretary of the union's executive committee. Clark advised Buchanan to accept the terms, but he refused. Clark then said he could probably get Adams to reinstate everyone but the secretary if Buchanan could accept that. Buchanan couldn't. On Monday, August 18, the seventh day of the strike, Adams offered to reinstate the secretary too if an investigation of his actions was "favorable." Buchanan said reinstate the secretary first and then conduct the investigation. At 4:00 P.M., Adams capitulated.

The affair was a stunning victory for the Knights of Labor. The union had not sought a second confrontation with the railroad, fearing it might not yet be strong enough, but when Adams forced a confrontation, the Knights rose to the occasion and triumphed. If they had been in any doubt about their strength before the strike, they weren't any longer.

It was only a matter of time now before coal miners caught the contagion. Already, back in June after the first shopmen's strike, colliers in Canon City, Colorado had struck the Canon City Coal Company, the local version of Beckwith Quinn, demanding cheaper supplies and the abolition of the ironclad. A month later, miners in two other Colorado camps—Erie and Louisville—likewise went out when their employer, the Colorado Coal Company, cut wages by 10 percent. Six hundred miners were now on strike in the Rockies. The two companies involved, contractors who sold their coal to the UP, rushed trainloads of Italian colliers to the scene to keep the mines operating.

Though there were local miners' assemblies in each of the three towns, there was no formal organization linking the strikers or any substantial strike fund. By mid-August, just as the walkouts were on the verge of collapse, the Knights won their second victory against the railroad, and the striking miners hit upon the idea of inviting Joseph Buchanan into the Rockies to work his magic in the coal camps. Buchanan accepted the invitation and organized several new locals under the order's banner. At the same time, he refused to call a wider strike and advised the miners to return to work; they should wait until winter, he explained, when demand was up and the company's position more vulnerable. He returned to Denver, promising, as he wrote in his memoirs, *The Autobiography of a Labor Agitator*, that "on the first day I look out my window and see snow on the foothills, I'll order the strike."[2] Meanwhile, to broaden his base, Buchanan sent one of his lieutenants, Thomas Neasham, to organize the coal camps in Wyoming and Montana.

Thus, thanks to the remarkable rise of the Knights of Labor, the stage was set for the first confrontation between coal miners and the UP since the debacle in Rock Springs a decade earlier.

The Knights of Labor was born one evening in early December 1869, when nine members of the former Garment Cutters Association of Philadelphia met in the home of Uriah Stephens and decided to found a new union. For two years, theirs was the only chapter, and it was not until 1874 that the first local outside Philadelphia, a gold beaters' assembly in New York, was organized. Soon after, as industrialization hit the shoe trade, shoemakers began flocking to the order and eventually became its largest single bloc. In 1876, the year the Miners National Association collapsed, the first colliers joined.

The union's slow growth, surprising at a time of great economic hardship, was due in part to its controversial new creed. The organization was not interested in becoming another glorified trade union; it meant to transcend—and bury—trade unionism altogether. The new member was not to think of himself as a cobbler, blacksmith, or brakeman, but simply as a wage earner, a man paid to work for another man, uniting with others of his kind to protect himself from the abuses of employers. Fragmented into trade unions—shoemakers, colliers, conductors—labor divided itself and was conquered; united as the Working Class, labor became a monopoly against the monopolies: "The Order tried to teach the American wage earner that he was a wage earner first and a bricklayer after; that he was a wage earner first and a Protestant, Catholic, Jew, white, black, Democrat, Republican after. This meant the Order was teaching something that was not so in the hope that some time it would be."[3]

While the order's message never caught on, the organization gradually attracted more and more members as the depression deepened until, during a brief period in the mid-1880s, it was arguably the most powerful force in the country.

The turnabout came during the stormy summer of 1877 when the Baltimore and Ohio and the Pennsylvania and New York Central railroads announced 10 percent wage cuts and touched off a week of anarchy across America. In Martinsburg, West Virginia, striking railroad workers overwhelmed civil authorities and held the town until two hundred federal troops arrived and restored order. In Baltimore, where an angry mob trapped federal troops in the armory, it was the police who rescued the army. Other riots racked Scranton, Harrisburg, Philadelphia, Buffalo, Toledo, Louisville, St. Louis, Chicago, and San Francisco (where the Central Pacific passed on the wage cut to its workers). The worst fighting was in Pittsburgh, where a National Guard contingent, some six hundred strong, fired on a crowd of striking railroad workers and killed twenty-six of them. Outraged strikers trapped the guardsmen in a roundhouse and forced railroad officials to order the guard to disband. The mob then went on a rampage through the city, destroying more than $5 million of railroad property.

Wage earners streamed into the order. By 1879, the size of the union had doubled, and one year later it had grown fivefold. Five months after the riots, the Knights of Labor held its first general assembly and established a national strike fund. The majority of the new members were miners and railroad workers, who now replaced shoemakers as the largest blocs, and the nation's railroads became the focus of the union's attention. The Knights' first successful strikes, in fact, were the two walkouts called against the Union Pacific in the summer of 1884.

These strikes represented a historic milestone in labor history: "For the first time in the history of the American labor movement," one historian wrote, "a union was able to deal with a modern corporation on terms of equality."[4] And the victories didn't hurt recruitment either; in only two years, membership climbed from 71,000 to 730,000, with several chapters overseas. The order, one writer noted, was "more observed than Congress," and one Washington newspaper even predicted the Knights would name the next president.

Snow fell in the Rockies on the night of October 24, and the next morning Joseph Buchanan, as good as his word, ordered a coal strike. The call went out for all miners in Colorado and Wyoming not to dig or load coal for the UP or its contractors unless the wage cut ordered back in July was rescinded. The strike was honored in Colorado and by miners in Carbon. In Rock Springs, where the colliers had not dared join the order, though some may have secretly, the men demonstrated their solidarity by destroying a ventilating fan and setting fire to the machine shop at Mine Number One. "All our tools are destroyed," the mine superintendent reported to Omaha, "together with many pump extras and fixtures. Our fan is destroyed; have made temporary arrangements for ventilation until such time as we receive new one. Had it happened in the summer, would have had to shut up the mine." But he wasn't advising capitulation: "If we give in now in Colorado, this organization will extend to all our mines; then we will have trouble."[5]

Charles Adams, who had expected the strike, was ready; he ordered the men at Carbon fired and directed Samuel Callaway, S. H. Clark's recent successor as general manager in Omaha, not to negotiate with the strikers or the union under any circumstances. "The policy of the directors is perfectly simple," he cabled. "We propose to be good tempered and reasonable, but entirely firm. Too much has already been yielded. They have beaten us twice under Clark's vacillating management. We are not going to yield one inch further."[6]

After several weeks, the miners in Colorado settled with the company, but the strike in Carbon, the UP's second most productive coal camp, dragged on into the new year. The miners, though they had been fired, kept the mines closed by threatening anyone who tried to work in their place. "They will not allow any man to work at the mines," Callaway reported to Adams in mid-January, "and they are most unreasonable in their demands." Chief among these, he noted, was that the UP should dismiss the "foreign labor" at Rock Springs.[7] The railroad refused.

A week later, the strike threatened to become more serious when Buchanan announced he was now prepared to call out the operating men, which would have crippled train service. "You are wrong," a flustered Callaway cabled Adams, "in your impression that [the strike] does not affect the operating department. Mr. Buchanan has taken the matter in hand and threatens all kinds of things. We are standing firm on our original proposition and waiting whatever medicine these gentlemen propose to give us. We seem to be constantly crawling through small holes. I hope to get through this one."[8]

Adams was not pleased with his new man in Omaha. "That poor, feeble, cowardly Callaway," he called him and soon fell into the habit of writing to men under Callaway to get what he considered a truer picture of affairs. Callaway, at thirty-five, had been working for one railroad or another since he was thirteen, but he was too cautious and timid for Adams's liking, an assessment shared by Oliver Ames, one of the government directors, who bemoaned Callaway's "lack of nerve and backbone."[9] Already Adams was deeply regretting his decision to place overall responsibility for day-to-day operations with the general manager in Omaha. He still believed in the principle of running the road from the field; he just didn't trust the man doing it.

In fairness to Callaway, it must be said that even a less cautious, more confident man would have hesitated when dealing with Adams, especially in a crisis. While Adams insisted tirelessly on Callaway's independence—"As regards closing the mine, you must decide" (September 16)—and the absurdity of trying to run the road from Boston—"I hold it would be perfect folly for one at this distance to undertake to direct operations" (September 20)—every cable and letter Adams wrote bristled with advice and specific instructions, often on the minutest of matters. And even on those increasingly rare occasions when Callaway did act on his own, more often than not he was brought up short by his mercurial boss. To no one's surprise, Callaway lasted only a year in the job.

"Be tough," Adams wired back regarding the impasse in Carbon. "There is no class of men out of whom the pluck and fight is more readily taken than strikers." He advised Callaway to get everything in writing and not to be so eager for the dispute to end, for it was generating a great deal of unfavorable publicity for the Knights. And as for the consequences of a prolonged stoppage, Callaway was not to worry: "If we go down, we go down together."[10]

"I have yours of 26 January," Callaway answered, "and am obliged by your expressions of confidence."[11]

Like his cables, Charles Francis Adams, the new man in Boston, was abrupt and combative. "I lack magnetism," he once confessed. "I am frightfully deficient in tact. I never could be a popular man."[12] He was abrasive, petulant, and insecure as well, and his accession to the presidency, with or without unions to serve as foils, portended an era of confrontation. He quarreled constantly with the railroad's board of directors, refused to take advice, and mistrusted and underestimated subordinates. "From his boyhood," wrote one anonymous detractor, "Charles manifested all the many signs of want of clearness of judgement that was hereafter to be the prominent trait of his character."[13]

Even Adams's family, by his own admission, could barely stand him. His sister-in-law, he observed, "never liked me...nor can I blame her. I trod all over her, offending her in every way." And his children, he went on, "were glad of any excuse that took them from home."[14] His mother was no less candid: "Nobody," she observed, "pays any attention to Charles."[15]

Of the famous Massachusetts Adamses, Charles spent his early years leading the life of the well-born dilettante, studying at Harvard, traveling on the continent, dabbling in several professions (including law and journalism), and, through his family, meeting most of the important men of the day. A detailed exposé of the men and the means surrounding a takeover of the Erie Railroad—the means were illegal, and the men included Jay Gould—won Adams some notoriety as a railroad expert and eventually led to his appointment as chairman of the Massachusetts Board of Railway Commissioners and later, in 1878, as one of the government directors of the UP. (In this capacity, he accompanied his two colleagues on the annual inspection tour of the road and thus came in frequent contact with what he later called "that great, fat, uninteresting West.") While his patrician upbringing and professional career may not have been the best preparation for running a major railroad with some fifteen thousand employees, most of them from the working class, trains were at least an avocation, and leadership, in any case, ran in the family.

On January 29, three months after the strike began, the miners in Carbon dropped their conditions and returned to work. But the victory was cold comfort for the company; violence had flared in Rock Springs, and the question of Chinese labor had emerged as an important issue. Nor could there be any doubt that the order would soon return to the contest and continue to score points off the Chinese question.

The company braced itself for the struggle ahead. "Radical

measures are necessary," Adams wrote Callaway, and immediately proposed two: no more white miners were to be hired in Rock Springs, not even to replace those who left, and all other vacancies along the line were, as far as possible, to be filled by Mormons. In the months that followed, forty new Chinese were hired in Rock Springs, and six whites were dismissed. Meanwhile, the company also cut back on operations at Carbon in order to minimize its dependence on that all-white camp.

Anticipating further violence, Adams ordered all company property insured and asked company lawyers to look into the question of whether, in the event of a strike, federal troops could be called in to protect property and employees. He was particularly worried about Wyoming where there was no territorial militia and the legality of using troops during the disturbances of 1875 had never been settled. Adams quite agreed with the assessment of the company's general solicitor on what to expect from the civil authorities in Wyoming; they "would be utterly powerless to cope with [strikers] even if they were inclined to. As a matter of fact, they are generally with the laborers."[16]

Throughout the spring, the Knights of Labor continued flexing its muscles, hitting the UP with an average of one strike every month, usually among the "operating men," such as conductors, brakemen, or firemen. And there was another miners' strike as well. "They now want to name the price at which we are to sell coal at Denver," Callaway reported. "They cannot do it without my consent." It was all getting to be too much for the general manager: "I confess to being entirely disheartened and discouraged," he continued, "and can see very little daylight ahead."[17] But he stood firm, and the Knights eventually backed down.

As the struggle heated up, the focus shifted increasingly toward Rock Springs, for the order could never hope to be effective in the coalfields so long as that town remained a virtual Chinese camp. There was also the growing fear that if the company didn't moderate its policies in Rock Springs soon, the white miners in that place, emboldened by labor agitation all around them, might take matters into their own hands. They could not help but be encouraged, for example, by the fact that a number of UP employees in Rock Springs who were not miners belonged to the order and held regular meetings in their own Knights of Labor hall. And there were persistent rumors that many colliers had secretly joined the union.

"It pains me greatly," John Lewis, with the order in Denver, wrote A. C. Beckwith that summer, "to have to call your attention to the fact that the Chinese problem at Rock Springs is assuming a grave attitude. There are nearly seventy-five of our men lying idle at the present time, while the Chinese are flooding in by the score. . . . Sensible as I am that unless a change is affected immediately there will be an outbreak, I respectfully notify you of the storm that is brewing."[18]

Terence Powderly, the Grand Master Workman (or chief) of the Knights of Labor, also pleaded with Beckwith to do what he could to defuse the tension in Rock Springs. "To my knowledge," Beckwith wrote in answer to Powderly's letter, "there has never been any complaint made by miners against the Union Pacific's coal department."[19]

During the summer, a rash of anti-Chinese violence broke out across the territory as the UP, in a fit of myopia, began replacing all whites on its section gangs with Chinese. Sojourners were threatened and beaten in Cheyenne and driven out of Rawlins and Laramie altogether. In the last week of August, posters suddenly appeared in Carbon, Rock Springs, and Evanston, warning all Chinese to leave the territory at once or face unspecified consequences. "The pressure is more than I can bear," Lewis wrote in a new plea to the superintendent of the Coal Department in Omaha. "The situation is terribly aggravating and will undoubtedly result in a severe struggle if longer continued. For God's sake do what you can to avoid this calamity."[20]

Throughout the month of August, two white miners, Isaiah Whitehouse and his partner William Jenkins, worked in entry 13 of Mine Number Six at Number Six Camp, Rock Springs. On the last day of the month, as was customary, mine superintendent Jim Evans closed all the entries and marked off new rooms. At the time, eight Chinese working in entry 5 were told by Evans that they would have to start in new rooms the following day. He then took one of the sojourners with him and pointed out the four new places he had marked off for them.

Later that same day, Evans encountered Whitehouse and Jenkins. He offered them the choice of staying where they were or choosing a new entry to work in. Knowing that entry 5 was the best in the pit, the two men asked to be moved there. Evans agreed but warned them to be careful to choose rooms beyond those already set aside for the Chinese.

The following morning, September 1, only four of the eight Chinese Evans had spoken to reported to the mine and, working in pairs, occupied only two of the four rooms that had been assigned to their crew. When Whitehouse and Jenkins arrived later, the pit boss told them to take the next two rooms beyond the Chinese, and the two men, taking one room each, set to work. Whitehouse stayed only three or four hours, long enough to set several charges in the rock face, and then left."

In the afternoon, there was an argument when the Chinese working next to Jenkins walked in on him and told him to leave. "I was driving where Mr. Whitehouse and his partner were working," a witness later testified before an inquiry chaired by the government directors: "Mr. Whitehouse went out in the forenoon and about noon the Chinamen came in and wanted his partner to get out; he said No, this was his room, and he was not going to get out; and they went into where Whitehouse had started and went to work in there. [Jenkins] told them it was Whitehouse's room. I heard him tell them this, and they said, 'No savee.' I also tried to persuade them not to go to work in there, but they said, 'No savee.'"[21]

The Chinese could not have picked a more influential miner to antagonize. Whitehouse, born in Staffordshire in the English coal country, emigrated with his parents to America when he was twenty and worked for a time in the Pennsylvania coalfields. He had lived in Rock Springs only two years, but he had already had his fair share of run-ins with the Chinese and the UP management, and he intended to do something about working conditions. The previous spring he had run for a seat in the territorial legislature, and with the near-unanimous support of his collier friends, he won handily. When the legislature convened the coming February, he had a long list of mining abuses he meant to raise, including the question Adams had mentioned about the legality of using U.S. troops to police the coalfields. In the meantime, as the delegate-elect from Sweetwater County, Whitehouse was in essence the de facto leader of the mining community. Little else is known about him, except that he was a family man, "of more than average intelligence,"[22] and not, in spite of his strong feelings, a radical.

On the evening of the first, a union meeting took place at the Knights of Labor hall in Rock Springs. In view of what transpired the following day, it was later widely alleged that the massacre of the Chinese was planned at this meeting. While there is no record of the proceedings, there is no other evidence to support this view, least of all the clumsy manner in which the massacre was carried out. Nor was there any need for planning; Chinatown was an easy target and the Chinese, in their isolation, completely unsuspecting. All the available evidence, on the contrary, strongly suggests that the massacre was not even intended, much less premeditated.

On the morning of September 2, 1885, the Chinese arrived early in entry 5, occupied Whitehouse's room as they had on the previous afternoon, and fired the charges he had set. When Whitehouse arrived, he found two sojourners clearing away the rubble:

> *Gov. Dir. Savage to Mr. Whitehouse*: When you went back to your room in the mine that day, and found the Chinamen there, you did not take any particular pains to find out whether it was a mistake?
>
> *Mr. Whitehouse*: I went in and sat down there for about half an hour, talking with the Chinamen in regard to their shaking the coal down and taking the place.... I asked [them] if they would only wait until the pit boss came; if he said they were to have the place, they could have it.[23]

But the Chinese were insistent. One of them became abusive, called Whitehouse a son of a bitch, and swung at him with his pick. Whitehouse hit back, knocking the man to the floor. The man screamed, and the noise brought several other Chinese running to the room. Whitehouse and Jenkins shouted for help as the Chinese closed in on them with picks, shovels, and tamping needles. A dozen white miners rushed to their aid while others blocked off the entry, pinning the Chinese in and keeping others out. A white foreman ran to get a pit car.

A man struck Whitehouse in the stomach with a pick. Several whites wrestled this sojourner to the ground and drove the pick three times into his skull. Six men surrounded another Chinese and beat him about the head with a shovel. Three other Chinese were severely beaten, and several whites were cut and bleeding about the head and face.

The fight lasted half an hour, broken off by the arrival of pit cars and several foremen. The Chinese laid their wounded in the cars, piled in after them, and were escorted past the white men to the mouth of the mine.

Above ground, word of the fight raced through Number Six Camp just as many miners were arriving at work. Ah Lip roused the pit boss, and Ah Koon, the number-two man in the Chinese community, ran into town to find mine superintendent Evans:

> *Gov. Dir. Savage to Ah Koon*: When did you first hear that there was

any trouble?

Ah Koon: About half-past nine. I hear there was trouble over in No. Six mine. I go down Rock Springs with China boy to office. I ask for Mr. Evans. I ask him,"You know trouble over in No. Six mine?" He say yes.

Mr. Evans: I hastened up to the mines and found most of the Chinamen out on top of the slope, and I told them to come down into the mines with me, and they came. When I got to No. 5 entry, all the white men were out ... waiting to go up in the cars. And I asked them what was the trouble, and some of them said that they were not going to suffer Chinamen to drive them out of the mines, and I asked them to come out of the cars and come to one side to reason the matter, that I thought it could all be settled very easily; but they would not listen. One of them cried out, "Come on, boys; we may as well finish it now, as long as we have commenced; it has to be done anyhow."[24]

Evans would not let the men go up in the pit cars, so they climbed out and started off on foot. As the miners were leaving, Evans took Whitehouse aside and asked him to go back to work. When he agreed, Evans asked him if he would try to persuade the others to return. "And he went and reported to me afterwards that he did so, but could not persuade any of them."[25]

The men went instead to their cabins at the nearby camp, armed themselves with guns, hatchets, clubs, and knives, and then reassembled on the tracks half a mile from Number Six. By this time, word of the fight had reached town, two miles west of the camp, and a citizens' committee was hastily formed and sent to talk with the miners, now reported to be making their way down the tracks toward the business district. The committee confronted the mob of colliers a mile east of Rock Springs, at the railroad bridge over Bitter Creek.

Mr. Zwicky: About one-half hour afterwards an armed body of men from No. Six came marching down the track toward the town. At the bridge crossing Bitter Creek the men halted and held a conference. Upon persuasion by a few citizens, they left their arms in the store nearby and continued their march up town and down Front Street towards the hall of the Knights of Labor, shouting, while marching, "White men fall in."[26]

The bell from the Knights of Labor hall rang out across the valley

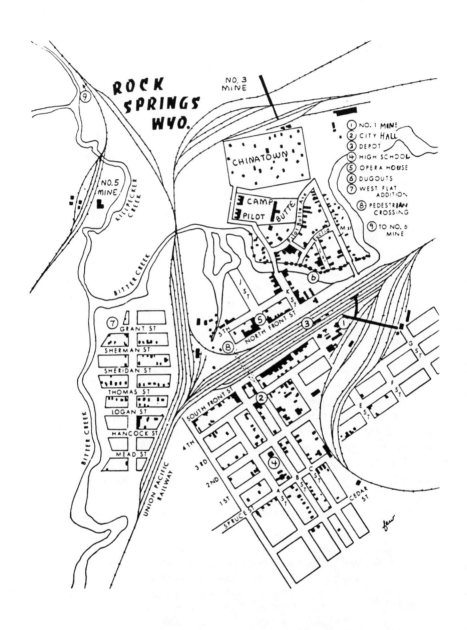

Rock Springs in the 1890s, showing Camp Pilot Butte and the new Chinatown. (Map by Frank E. Wright, from Booms and Busts on Bitter Creek, *Pruett Publishing Co., Boulder, Colorado)*

to announce a special meeting, and men from the nearest mines were soon assembled. The men from Number Six told their story, and a vote was then taken to hold another general meeting that evening at six o'clock.

After the morning meeting broke up, most of the colliers crowded into the saloons along Front Street. As word of the trouble spread into outlying camps, more miners walked off the job and gathered in town. At noon, alarmed at the ugly mood of their customers, saloon keepers kicked the miners out and closed the taverns. Many other shops were also closing.

The men mingled in the streets, shouting anti-Chinese slogans. A few sojourners, unaware of the trouble, passed through town on their way home for lunch, and groups of boys and men hurled chunks of coal and brickbats at them, chased and kicked them, and fired shots just above their heads. Nothing like this had ever been seen before in Rock Springs; it was evident by noon that something quite extraordinary was under way, that a corner had been turned, and that whatever else happened that day—and no one had any idea what that might be—life in the town would never be the same again.

There was still no alarm in Chinatown, a mile down the tracks to the east. September 2 was a Chinese holiday, and many Orientals had not gone to work. The first they heard of the trouble was when David Thomas, mine superintendent at Number Five, passed through Hong Kong at midmorning "notifying five or six of my Chinese friends to be careful as it looked like trouble was brewing."[27] "As yet," the Chinese explained in their affidavit on the massacre, later presented to the Chinese minister in Washington, "the mob had not come to attack the Chinese. A great number of the latter were returning to work without any apprehension of danger."[28]

A little after 2:00 P.M., a rumor swept through the crowd on Front Street that railroad officials had wired for federal troops to come and put down any disturbances. The crowd now numbered between 100 and 150, most of them armed, and included not only coal miners but many railroad workers as well as assorted other individuals who had either a grudge against the Chinese or a taste for violence. Spurred into action by the rumor, the mob started off for Chinatown, followed by a crowd of curious onlookers, including numerous women and children.

The mob marched east along the tracks, on the south side of Bitter Creek. Passing the King, Gagen, and Mathews firearms store, the men stopped and bought out the entire stock of ammunition. Next they bore down on a section house beside the tracks and routed the half-dozen frightened Orientals cowering inside, scattering them with warning shots.

Now the rioters reached the first of the two bridges over the creek, where they stopped to confer. A three-man delegation then proceeded over the bridge and into Chinatown to notify the Chinese that they had one hour to pack their belongings and leave town.

At last the Chinese began to awake to their danger. "All was excitement in Chinatown; the [red] flag was hoisted as a warning and the Chinamen gathered to their quarters from all parts of town."[29] The sojourners could just make out the mob half a mile down the tracks on the opposite side of the river. Even then, most of the Chinese did not heed the warning of the delegation, as they observed in their affidavit: "About two o'clock the mob suddenly made their appearance for the attack. The Chinese thought they had only assembled to threaten and that some of the company officials would come to disperse them. Most of the Chinese, acting on this view of the matter, did not gather up their money or clothing."[30]

After forty-five minutes, a new rumor spread through the mob: The Chinese were arming themselves and barricading their homes. The rioters decided to march on Chinatown at once. Here the men split into two groups, one crossing the bridge they now stood in front of and advancing along the north side of the tracks, the other group marching in a parallel column down the south side and crossing by the larger railroad bridge immediately east of Chinatown, at the foot of the hill leading up to Mine Number Three.

The first group stormed over the bridge, posted guards to seal off any Chinese escape, and advanced cautiously toward Hong Kong. The second group, meanwhile, upon gaining the railroad bridge, split into three squads: one each to guard either side of the bridge and a third that now crossed the river and made the first attack of the afternoon, charging up the hill at Mine Number Three and firing on the Chinese hiding in the coal shed and pump house.

One of the first to fall was Lor Sun Kit, routed out by the gang at the pump house and shot through the back as he fled. Leo Dye Bah fell next as he ran down the hill straight into the squad at the railroad bridge. He took a bullet in the chest and tumbled dead into the creek. Leo Kow Boot made a dash for Mine Number Four and was killed by a bullet through the neck. By an unfortunate coincidence, four of the Chinese wounded during the fighting at Number Six in the morning had been taken to Number Three for treatment. Only one of them was ever seen again.

Across the creek, the crowd of onlookers grew larger, many climbing onto boxcars to get a better view, cheering and urging on the rioters:

> *Mr. Zwicky*: Soon the rioters came abreast of the outlying houses of Chinatown, about 100 strong, half of them carrying Winchester rifles. There they halted, as it seemed, for consultation. In a little while several revolver shots were fired, whether by whites or Chinamen I could not say. The rioters now cautiously advanced. Now a rifle shot, followed by another and still another, and then a volley was fired. The Chinamen were fleeing like a herd of hunted antelope, making no resistance. Volley upon volley was fired after the fugitives. In a few minutes the hill east of town was literally blue with hunted Chinamen. What [had] appeared at first to be the mad frolic of ignorant men was turning into an inhuman butchery of innocent beings.[31]

After the shootings at Number Three, that squad linked up with the group that had crossed at the plank bridge, and a combined force of eighty to one hundred men now marched on Chinatown proper. As they reached the western edge of the settlement, the rioters broke into groups of eight or ten and fanned out into the narrow streets and cramped alleyways. Some Chinese darted from their cabins and were immediately cut down. Others hid in their homes until they were routed out and forced to flee through the streets. Still others, in a fatal miscalculation, hid undetected in their cellars.

"Like a flock of frightened sheep,"[32] said one paper; "like a herd of hunted antelopes,"[33] said another—the Chinese fled. Unarmed, bare-headed, barefoot, wearing only their flimsy cotton jackets and pants, they darted from house to house, carrying what they could in a bedroll or a bandanna. Most carried nothing at all, not even their money. As they had just been paid at the end of the month, looters would not be disappointed.

They fled in every direction; west toward Mine Number Three and then north toward the bottom of the rock butte behind Chinatown; straight west toward the plank bridge and on across toward Rock Springs; or, the majority, southeast, just ahead of the mob, down the twenty-foot bank of Bitter Creek, through the water, up the other side, across the tracks, and on through the sagebrush and greasewood toward Burning Mountain and the hills south of town. A few carried wives and children. Some, under the influence of rice wine or opium after celebrating the holiday, stumbled about in dazed confusion.

Many ran straight into marauding gangs of rioters. Some were merely robbed of their watches, jewels, gold, and money, and told to run. Others were beaten with rifles and clubs, robbed, and left bleeding in the dirt. Others were shot.

Ah Say, the venerable leader of the Chinese community, fled with Leo Chee, custodian of all UP stock and barns. Ah Say was wounded and fell. Leo Chee reversed direction and fled west toward Green River, some twelve miles distant, arriving there, the story goes, ahead of a train that left Rock Springs at the same time he did. Ah Say managed to crawl off and was eventually picked up and taken to Evanston.

His assistant, Ah Koon, had a close call as well:

> *Ah Koon:* Three or four white men came along and kick door and say, "You better come out or we drag you out." I come out and run about two hundred yards. I turn my head, I look back and see three or four white men standing. He see me and shot me four times. I fall down and drop the money and ran. I went down the track across the river. I walk up to railroad section house, knock at door, and say, "Mr., you better open door and let me in." He say, "Who's that?" I say, "China boy." He open the door and let me come into that house. I say, "I am nearly dead, I got nothing to eat." I ask him, "You give me some bread?" He say, "You got some bread." He say, "What's the matter at Rock Springs?" I say, "Lots trouble, drive China boys out."[34]

Ah Koon left $1,600 and his famous fur coat behind.

One of the most prominent and visible rioters was a doctor, the flamboyant Edward Murray, who rode a horse up and down Chinatown at the height of the massacre, waving his hat and urging on the mob. "No quarter!" he yelled. "Shoot them down." His behavior was later attributed to the fact that he wanted very much to become the Coal Department's doctor and was trying to ingratiate himself with the miners.

There were several women out that day too, most notably a pair attached to the gang guarding the railroad bridge. Yee See Yen was shot in the head by one of the ladies, and two other sojourners were fatally wounded in the chest by her partner. This latter woman also wounded another man in the thigh, and he subsequently lay bleeding through the night by the side of the river. Another woman, a Mrs. Osborn, proprietress of a local laundry, was part of one of the gangs roaming through Hong Kong. She was widely credited with killing two Chinese with only three shots. "She was not only unmolested," noted a reporter from the New York *Evening Post*, "but is applauded for her public spirit."[35] "The women handled weapons like men, and used them too. One, who had a child in her arms, struck a passing Mongol and knocked him down. The baby screamed, and she spanked it, laid it on the ground and proceeded to smash [the Chinaman] in regular John L. Sullivan style."[36]

Several fleeing Chinese threw themselves at the mercy of whites whom they trusted. Eleanor Thirloway, daughter of the Reverend and Mrs. Timothy Thirloway, tutored a number of Chinese in English and "frequently wrote notes" for them. At the height of the rioting, the Thirloways suddenly found five or six terrified Chinese on their doorstep. They "asked for shelter," Eleanor later told the grand jury, "but we thought they would not be safe and advised them to leave town as others were doing."[37] Eleanor was observed later that evening picking over the loot in Chinatown. Several other sojourners were taken in by white friends and hidden until the violence was over. One hid in the basement of the Beckwith Quinn store for a week.

The mob finished its first sweep through Chinatown by four o'clock and regrouped at the eastern edge of the settlement. Dead and wounded Chinese lay strewn about the street, along the riverbank, and in the creek itself. Burning Mountain, to the southeast, was covered with those who had fled: "They were scattered far and near, high and low, standing or sitting or lying hid in the grass or stooping down on the low grounds, everyone of them praying to Heaven or groaning with pain."[38]

But many Chinese had not fled, hiding in their homes instead, and were now flushed out as the rioters, at Dr. Murray's suggestion, made a second pass through Hong Kong to set fire to the buildings and thereby guarantee that the Chinese would not return. As fire swept through their cabins, the sojourners burst into the street, their heads wrapped in bedrolls and blankets to protect them from the smoke and flames within and the bullets without. Some retreated into their cellars rather than risk running the gauntlet outside and thereby reserved for themselves the grisliest fate of the afternoon. Leo Chih Ming, Liang Tsun Bong, and Hsu Ah Cheong shared a UP hut near the temple in the center of Hong Kong. Trapped by flames in their cellar, they clawed desperately at the earthen walls to make a hole they could crawl into. But they didn't have enough time, and the holes were too shallow; only the head and chest of Leo Chih Ming were recovered; the hands, shoulders, and head of Liang Tsun Bong; and the skull of Hsu

Ah Cheong.

Next door, two other Chinese met the same end. China Joe was luckier; he hid in his oven for three days and later escaped. Another sojourner, cowering in his privy, was discovered by the mob, dragged outside, and tossed into the flames of a burning house. Many of the bodies lying in the streets were also tossed into the fire.

Forty dwellings were ablaze. The flames leapt from house to house, the shacks made of building paper catching quickly in a great roar, the wooden UP cabins burning slowly and steadily. From time to time an explosion rocked the afternoon as the flames found the kegs of gunpowder miners stored in their cabins, and bits of wood, crockery, metal, glass, earth—and Chinese—descended in a soft hail. Across the river, each explosion was greeted with a great cheer from the assembled crowd. A black cloud rose skyward, and the stench of burning flesh drifted over the valley.

With Chinatown empty and on fire, the mob split up to visit each of the mines surrounding Rock Springs and run off any Chinese who might still be hiding out. The small Chinese camps at Number Six and Number Three were empty, but they were both put to the torch anyway. "From here the rioters went to No. One Mine. A few poor wretches had sought safety there, but they were driven out while the rioters fired their rifles into the air. It was too public a place for any rioter to aim low."[39]

The main body of men now marched back across the river and advanced on the laundry owned by Ah Lee:

> There was no sign of a Chinaman here at first, but a vigorous search revealed one hidden away in a corner. But he would not dare to come out. Then the roof was broken in, and shots fired to scare him out, but a shot in return showed that the Chinaman was armed. A rush through the door followed, then came a scuffle, and a number of shots; and looking through an opening, a dead Chinaman was seen on the floor with blood and brains oozing from a terrible wound in the back of his head.[40]

Mrs. Osborn, the laundress who had already killed two Chinese in Hong Kong, stepped over the body and began looting the clothes. Another woman in the crowd, said to have lost a child only a day or so before, jumped up and down on the corpse.

The mob had three more items of business: to call at the homes of three UP officials closely associated with the hiring of Chinese. The first was the Chinese boss Soo Qui, who lived in style in a company house at the eastern edge of Rock Springs. The mob surrounded the house and demanded that Soo show himself. But Soo had already fled, though his wife for some reason had not, and she now "came to the door much terrified, and with tearful eyes and trembling voice, said: 'Soo he go. I go to him.' "[41] But it was Soo they wanted, a spokesman explained, not her. She was welcome to stay. When they left, she gathered up her belongings and was taken in by a neighbor. When she finally departed three days later, "dressed in the height of Celestial style, abounding in gorgeous colors, [carrying] a handsome fan and other feminine accoutrements," Mrs. Soo was the last of her race to leave Rock Springs.[42]

Next the mob visited the shop of W. H. O'Donnell, a local butcher who had just recently become Beckwith's agent in charge of procuring Chinese miners. Many in the crowd were sympathetic toward O'Donnell. The man who killed Ah Lee quit the mob at this point, "highly indignant at the treatment meted out to the butcher," but the majority prevailed. O'Donnell's teamster faced down the mob from the doorstep of the shop and was given a note for his employer: "Mr. O'Donnell," it said, "You must not bring anymore Chinamen to this town. Leave as soon as possible."[43] He left on the next train.

The last stop was the home of Jim Evans, the unpopular mine superintendent at Number Six. Evans watched from inside as the rioters approached: "They surrounded the house in which I was boarding and asked if Evans was in. I heard them and went out and asked them if they wished to see me; and one by the name of Allen Roberts said that they had come to the conclusion to ask me to leave town, and that they did not want to hurt me and that they would give me from then until the train came in to go. It was then near six o'clock, and the train left at twenty minutes past seven o'clock. So I left when the train came in."[44]

Evans, unlamented, was never seen in Rock Springs again.

It was now dusk, and many of the rioters went home for supper or joined the crowd of looters descending on Chinatown. Eleanor Thirloway was there, picking through the handkerchiefs, and another woman found Ah Koon's well-known fur coat and was making off with it. (Several days later she tried to sell the coat to a Mrs. Thayer, saying it was made from the skin of an African lion, but Mrs. Thayer recognized the garment and refused to buy it.) Many whites were digging in the rubble of burned-out houses, looking for buried gold. Others dragged heavy metal trunks into the streets and rifled the contents. Boys chased chickens, ducks, geese, and pigs through the narrow passageways. One boy carried a pig around his neck; another made off with one under his arm; a third was running one wheelbarrow-fashion down the street, mumbling in answer to a question, "Do you think I'm going to fight all day for nothing?"[45]

David Thomas and two friends took a walk through Chinatown at this hour, "the flames from forty burning houses lighting our faces."[46] Food, bedding, clothing, stoves, crockery, opium pots, gin bottles, and furniture littered the streets. Dogs, pigs, and fowl feasted on boiled turnips, roasted fish, angleworms, and chunks of cooked cabbage. Thomas came across an old Chinese he knew, bleeding to death through a wound in the chest. The men struggled with the

David Thomas, mine superintendent at Number Five and friend of the Chinese. (Photograph from The Sweetwater County Historical Museum, Green River, Wyoming)

thought of shooting the man to stop his suffering, but no one could bring himself to pull the trigger. Further east they came across four corpses—one in the creek, his face upturned—and they also encountered three wounded Chinese whom they arranged to have taken into town and treated. Later, near the end of their walk, they passed a hog mutiliating a corpse, "and for a long time," Thomas wrote, "pork was not tempting."[47]

After supper, the rioters reassembled, only fifty or so now, to complete the burning of Chinatown. Fifty houses, half of Hong Kong, still stood. Bearing torches, the men crossed the creek and one by one set them all aflame. The great fire lit up the faces of the watching crowd and the great rock butte that loomed behind Chinatown. Keg after keg of gunpowder exploded, sending burning embers hundreds of feet into the air "as if from the center of a volcano,"[48] and the sound of rolling thunder echoed across the valley. Out on the prairie, shivering in the frosty night air, more than five hundred sojourners watched Chinatown burn slowly to the ground.

Later that evening, a miner sat in his cabin writing a letter to his wife in Salt Lake City. "Since noon today," he began, "we've had an exciting time."[49]

6

A Condition of War

Unless [you] can find way to relieve us immediately, I believe worse scenes than those at Rock Springs will follow...I beg an early reply and information regarding attitude of the U.S. Government.
—GOVERNOR FRANCIS WARREN *to President Cleveland*

SEPTEMBER 2. Rock Springs had no source of potable water. Every afternoon at three o'clock, a water train left for Green River, twelve miles west. As the seat of Sweetwater County, Green River was also the site of the closest sheriff, one Joseph Young. As the water train was leaving on the afternoon of September 2, a Union Pacific official handed a note to the conductor and asked him to pass the message on to the sheriff. The note told Young of the trouble in Rock Springs, now barely an hour old, and asked him to form a posse and come at once to the scene.

At the same time, a cable was sent to James Tisdale, superintendent of the mines at Rock Springs, who had accompanied his wife to a teachers' convention in Cheyenne. Tisdale received the cable at 5:00 P.M. and went immediately to the office of Governor Warren. Warren in turn wired General Howard, commander of the Department of the Platte in Omaha.

Wyoming had no territorial militia. Aside from a number of sheriffs and U.S. marshals scattered across the various counties, there was no organized peacekeeping force at the governor's disposal in case of an emergency. Only the U.S. Army, garrisoned in several forts sprinkled around the territory, could handle a major outbreak of violence, and then only on orders from General Howard.

Warren's first cable alerted the general about possible trouble in

Governor Francis Warren (Photograph from Wyoming State Archives, Museums and Historical Department, Cheyenne)

Rock Springs, but made no request for assistance. At 5:00 P.M., Warren received a message from Sheriff Young, now at the scene: "There is a riot in Rock Springs between white and Chinese miners. It is necessary that the same should be suppressed, and I call on you to send two companies of soldiers to Rock Springs immediately."[1]

Young, who had come by special train from Green River, arrived in Rock Springs just before the rioters went home for dinner. He was on hand, then, for the mob's second sweep through Chinatown in the evening but was unable to prevent it. He later claimed that he had tried to organize a posse but that everyone he approached was either in sympathy with the mob or afraid to cross them. Worried about his own safety, he posted a few guards in front of key UP buildings and got out of sight. Warren later strongly criticized Young's actions: "If Joe Young had had a particle of courage, the matter of burning of buildings, loss of life, etc. would have been prevented or greatly lessened."[2]

Governor Warren wired General Howard again, this time requesting troops, and then rode out to Fort Russell, three miles from Cheyenne, to brief Colonel Mason and to ask him to put his men on alert.

The first news of the riot reached the offices of the UP in Omaha just as they were about to close for the day. Thomas Kimball, the general traffic manager, sent an urgent plea to the governor: "If you have not sufficient civil force at your command to protect this company's property and employees at Rock Springs, will you not immediately telegraph General Howard to send you aid at once. If necessary for you to consult the Secretary of War, please wire him immediately."[3]

Meanwhile, company brass converged on Cheyenne from all directions. Superintendent Toohey was ordered to proceed from Denver, and Callaway dispatched General Superintendent Dickinson and Superintendent Wurtele of the western division from Omaha. The three officials rendezvoused in Cheyenne just after 11:00 P.M. and hurried to the capitol to consult with the governor and Tisdale. The governor, in the meantime, had wired the secretary of war.

The men conferred until midnight, then proceeded to the station and boarded a special train for Rock Springs. At 1:30 A.M., as the train stopped for refueling, a message was handed to the governor in his car. The cable, from General Howard's assistant, informed Warren that his troop request had been forwarded to division headquarters in Chicago "for instructions" but that troops were now on alert at Fort Russell, near Cheyenne, and at Fort Steele, 108 miles east of Rock Springs. "I suggest," Adjutant Breck concluded, "that you apply by telegraph to the President, at Washington."[4]

From Washakie, the next telegraph station west, Warren wired the president:

> An armed body of white men at Rock Springs, Wyoming have attacked Chinese coal miners working for Union Pacific Railway at that point. Have driven Chinamen out of town into hills. Have burned their houses and are destroying railroad property. Three men known to have been killed, many more believed to be. Mob now preventing some five-hundred Chinamen from reaching food or shelter. Sheriff of county powerless to suppress riot and asks for two companies United States troops. I believe immediate assistance imperative to preserve life and property.[5]

SEPTEMBER 3. The dignitary-laden train pulled into Rock Springs just after dawn. "The stench of burning human flesh was sickening and almost unendurable," Warren later wrote,

> and was plainly discernible for more than a mile along the railroad both east and west. Nearly a score of the dead bodies of Chinamen (or the dismembered parts of bodies enough to make that number) had been picked up where shot on the plains or had been exhumed from the ashes and from the earth that had fallen in from the dirt roofs where they had been roasted to death in their own homes, and the opinion prevailed that fully as many more were yet under the ruins. Not a living Chinaman—man, woman, or child—was left in the town where 700 to 900 had lived the day before, and not a single house, shanty, or structure of any kind that had ever been inhabited by a Chinaman was left unburned.[6]

An eerie quiet hung over Rock Springs, now in complete control of the mob. Businesses were closed, the mines idle. All trains sped past without stopping. Company officials stayed indoors while outside armed rioters patrolled the streets. A delegation met with the governor and warned him, in his words,

> that no Chinese should ever again live in Rock Springs, that no one should be arrested for acts committed, and that danger and destruction would attend all those who might choose to differ with them.
>
> The town was so terrorized at this time that scarcely a dozen people in it could be found who would offer a word in condemnation of the occurrence, the balance being either silent, non-committal, or in sympathy with the rioters.[7]

For the sojourners, the situation was desperate. The temperature dropped below freezing the night of the second, and several Chinese had already died from exposure. Others, wounded in flight, might also die if they did not get medical attention at once. Many Chinese were not even wearing shirts, having fled directly from the mines, where they often worked barechested. Later in the week, stories began trickling in of the ordeal many Chinese had faced out on the prairie. You Kwang told how he and five others got lost in the hills and wandered for two days. Separated from his friends, You finally stumbled across the railroad tracks and was saved. His friends were never seen again. Another group of five sojourners became lost and ate their own excrement to survive. Four of them eventually died anyway, too weak to fend off the wolves, and a fifth, Pang Chung, chased by the predators, staggered into Rock Springs. The saddest tale, carried by several newspapers in the East, was of the family—mother, father, one child—who fled across Burning Mountain and into wild country southeast of town. The infant died in a few hours from dehydration and the next day the mother succumbed to exposure. As wolves circled, the crazed father shot himself.

Chinese who approached the outskirts of town on the third were driven off with warning shots. Another day and night without water and shelter would mean death to scores of Chinese. Many had found the tracks and followed them west to Green River and were now huddled on an island in the middle of the stream, occasionally menaced by Knights who watched from the banks. Taking charge of the situation, Governor Warren asked the company to outfit two trains with food and blankets, and send one in each direction to rescue any Chinese found along the tracks. At the same time, conductors of regularly scheduled trains were asked to pick up any Chinese they encountered, and volunteers were sent into the hills with food and blankets. Even then, when the rescue operation was over, more Chinese had died in the hills after the massacre than during the rioting.

As they were picked up, the Chinese were transported to Evanston, ninety miles west of Rock Springs, and taken in by their countrymen in the large Chinatown on the edge of the white community. These Chinese, most of whom worked for the Central Pacific, also included a contingent who worked for the UP mine at Almy, three miles outside of town. By late afternoon on the third, close to five hundred sojourners had been found and brought to Evanston. As they marched through town from the railway station, they bought out the entire stock of several gun and ammunition shops.

Governor Warren spent the morning and afternoon of the third in Rock Springs, conferring with company officials and Sheriff Young. While he stayed most of the time in a private car on a siding near Front Street, he made a point of emerging from time to time to show himself to the mob. "It was most fortunate," the great Western historian Hubert Bancroft later wrote, "that at this juncture a man of [Warren's] determined character was at the head of affairs."[8]

Francis E. Warren, married, father of two, expected daily to lose his job. A Republican in a Democratic administration, he ought to have been replaced months earlier when Grover Cleveland assumed the presidency, but Cleveland had moved slowly on the appointment—in spite of vigorous protests from Wyoming's Democrats that if he didn't act soon the party would be "too dead to bury"—until now, in the midst of a crisis, it was too late. Warren's handling of the Rock Springs affair launched him on a distinguished national career, culminating in nearly three decades of service as a U.S. senator, then a record, during which time, as chairman of the Senate Appropriations Committee, he was one of the most powerful men in Washington.

Originally from Massachusetts, Warren came west as a construction foreman on the Rock Island Railway and later moved to Cheyenne where he established the Francis E. Warren Mercantile Co., the cornerstone of what was to become the largest financial empire in Wyoming. In 1884, he was elected mayor of Cheyenne, and a year later President Arthur appointed him governor.

Politically conservative and allied with the business interests—he also had railroad investments—he was not anxious for organized labor to gain a foothold in the territory. "During the last two years," he wrote Callaway shortly after the massacre, "I have been constantly annoyed at the growing disposition of labor to entirely rule capital in this vicinity. I believe it kinder to the working man [if companies] make no concessions; repeated softenings encourage impudent demands."[9] On another occasion, he wrote UP President Charles Adams that "labor must be subordinate to the employing power to insure law and order in our territory."[10]

All the same, he was strongly opposed to the use of Chinese labor, whose presence he felt retarded the growth of Wyoming. Yet he knew his duty: "It is not necessary for me to say to those who know me that I have no fondness for Chinese . . . but I do have an interest in protecting, as far as in my power lies, the lives, liberty, and property of every human being in this territory . . . and so long as I am governor, I shall act in the spirit of that idea."[11]

Warren was a big man, with long sideburns and a flowing handlebar mustache, and an excellent orator, sprinkling his speeches with statistics and literary allusions. He was awarded the Congressional Medal of Honor for courage under fire at the Battle of Port Hudson and never appeared in public without the decoration pinned to his lapel. His motto was "Never hunt ducks with a brass band."

As a reporter from the New York *Evening Post* observed Warren's dealing with the rioters in Rock Springs on the afternoon of the third, he was impressed with the governor's bravery: "He is a young, energetic man of commanding presence and determination of character.

A less courageous man might have hesitated about exposing himself."[12]

Warren controlled himself during these face-offs with the rioters, but privately he seethed. When he was asked his opinion of the affair several days later, he responded "vehemently": "It is the most brutal and damnable outrage that ever occurred in any country. Those fellows actually attacked the Chinese in their own abodes while they were packing to get away, shot them unresistingly and pushed them back into the shanties and roasted them like so many rats. . . . [Some of these] assailants were miners, who are the dregs of the lowest order of immigrants, ignorant and brutal by nature, never having had an opportunity to learn any better than to be led into such performances."[13]

The headquarters of the UP in Omaha was the old reconstructed Herndon Hotel, a four-story building near the center of the city. The general manager's office, in the southwest corner of the first floor, was one of two elaborately furnished show offices, complete with plate-glass windows, a Brussels carpet, a large rolltop desk, a swivel chair, and pictures of scenic wonders along the line. Throughout the day on the third, Callaway sat at his desk, alternately talking with reporters and reading cables handed to him every few minutes by a clerk who worked at a small desk in one corner.

The reporters pressed Callaway for a statement of the company's view of the massacre. "This is certainly an unfortunate occurrence," he declared, "but the Union Pacific is so . . . blameless that it is scarcely concerned except in the anxiety for its exposed property and the desire to resume the operation of the mines now idle. I am unable to state now what will be done about labor in the future, as the end of the difficulty must be seen before any plans can be devised."[14]

If the company was also anxious about the Chinese, Callaway didn't say so.

As Callaway pieced together what happened, he sent frequent updates on the situation to Adams. His first cable reported one death, an injured child, and the burning of "houses." By noon, the death toll had climbed to fourteen and the number of burned houses to one hundred. Still another wire put the death count at fifteen, with as many more bodies believed to be buried in the ruins. "Six-hundred Chinese are scattered through the Territory," he continued. "The local authorities are wholly powerless, and the city is in the hands of a mob. Governor Warren is asking for troops and requests that you communicate with the President."[15]

By the end of the day, the worst of the crisis seemed to have passed. The killing and burning had stopped in Rock Springs, most of the Chinese had been rescued, and troops, it was assumed, would soon be on their way. Warren accordingly left Rock Springs in the early evening and proceeded to Green River for the night. In the morning, he planned to go on to Evanston to inspect arrangements there and confer with A. C. Beckwith.

"While there," Warren later wrote of his night in Green River, "I received a telegram from the sheriff of Uinta county (the next western county) in which is situated the Almy coal mines . . . near the town of Evanston. In this place were assembled the five hundred or so Chinese living there and the Chinese refugees from Rock Springs:

For Governor Warren, Green River:

In the opinion of the prominent citizens of Evanston and myself the outrages at Rock Springs are liable to be repeated here. The property and lives of some of our citizens [are] in great danger, as well as the property of the Union Pacific Railway Company. Over 500 Chinese refugees from Rock Springs are here now. I would respectfully request the aid of a company of troops immediately.
      Can you come up tomorrow?"[16]

SEPTEMBER 4. Warren went to Evanston the following morning and "found the situation very serious, an outbreak seeming imminent."[17] "The saloons were closed," wrote another eyewitness,

and deputies placed on guard to protect railroad property, while knots of men gathered about the streets, discussing the situation in whispers. It was estimated that there was not more than fifteen men in the place, including county and railroad officials who would turn their hand to save the persecuted Orientals.
      Ah Say was met by the writer Thursday evening. He was extremely nervous and his conversation evidenced intense agitation. He was urgent in his appeals to Superintendent Dickinson to provide for the [Chinese].[18]

Warren cabled the latest to General Howard and then added: "I fear further trouble all along the line. What instructions have you regarding my request [for troops]?"[19]

Warren's fears were realized almost at once. Trouble broke out in

Green River on the heels of his departure, and word reached him later that morning that the mob in Rock Springs had ordered Mine Superintendent Tisdale to leave town and then broken into the boarded-up Beckwith Quinn powder house and picked it clean. There was also trouble that morning at company mines in Grass Creek, Utah, the next camp beyond Evanston, where members of the order gave the Chinese who worked there twenty minutes to leave. The slowly spreading stain of civil unrest now covered more than 150 miles of southwest Wyoming and Utah, and the number of threatened Chinese was rapidly approaching twelve hundred. "It is argued," noted one observer, "that surely there must be some law-abiding citizens in the [region]. There may be, but they are not in sight."[20]

There was one, however—a Mrs. O. J. Johnson, the proprietress of the Deseret Hotel in Green River. On the third, the day after the massacre, members of the Knights informed her that she must dismiss all the Chinese who worked for her and at the same time ordered the Chinese to leave town by nightfall. Mrs. Johnson refused, gathered all the Chinese inside the hotel, and posted a guard outside. The next day,

> I sent for the Knight in charge here, and I guess I talked for he afterwards said he thought a cyclone had struck him. He said he had not authorized anyone to send [the Chinese] away and was sorry such had been done. . . . He said the only thing they would do would be to boycott the house. . . . I told him that while we should regret such an affair we would still run the house. Many came in to talk of it (sent I felt sure); and to one and all I said that I did not mean to allow any one to run the house and that I would keep the boys.
>
> [In the] evening one of the men that chased the Chinamen came into the office and sat down. He was half drunk and ugly. I was called out for a minute and when I came back I found him going out in the back part of the house. I asked him what he wanted and he said he was just looking round. I took him by the shoulder and told him to look round outside and walked him out of doors.[21]

"It's a great pity," Adams said of her, "some of the men in that region do not have as much courage as this woman."[22] In the end, though the Knights backed down; most of the Green River Chinese asked the railroad for passes and joined the swelling ranks of their countrymen in Evanston.

The key role played by members of the order in these incidents led to the widespread belief that the anti-Chinese violence in the Rockies was all part of a carefully coordinated plan masterminded by the union leadership in Denver. But there was no such campaign; while the union certainly supported the expulsion of the Chinese, it was strongly opposed to the use of force or violence. The incidents at Green River, Evanston, Grass Creek, and several isolated section houses along the line were merely ripples from the stone cast at Rock Springs and, like the massacre itself, were essentially the work of individuals—many of whom happened also to be Knights—carrying out their own private vendettas against the sojourner without either the approval or the knowledge of the order. The union would be drawn into the affair soon enough, but it played no part in its conception.

Adams and Callaway spent the fourth trying to raise the government in Washington. "If troops are not furnished immediately," Callaway wrote Adams regarding the crisis in Evanston, "there can be no question but that the entire Chinese population along our line will be driven away."[23] Adams cabled the secretary of war.

The company's concern at that hour was to protect its property and its white employees, and to reopen its mines as soon as possible. An estimated $5,000 in property had already been destroyed, and over $1 million more was threatened. Meanwhile, scores of coal contracts representing hundreds of thousands of dollars were also jeopardized. Countless businesses along the line would be hurt or crippled without timely deliveries of coal, and ultimately the company's ability to run its own trains would be affected. Already, in his second cable concerning the riot, Adams was asking Callaway, "How will Rock Springs affair affect your contracts for coal delivery?"[24]

"Operations at Rock Springs almost entirely suspended," Callaway answered, "cannot form any estimate of our ability to carry out coal contracts. . . . At present our property is in hands of mob and our officers have been obliged to leave town. [General Superintendent] Dickinson thinks we had better close all the mines, but I fear this would result in spreading the trouble to shops and cause further destruction of property. We should know quick as possible if we are to have any protection from United States Government."[25]

In Evanston, where Sheriff LeCain now had thirty deputies guarding Chinatown and the most important railroad buildings, Governor Warren was wondering the same thing. In the afternoon, now two full days after his first call for troops, Warren got an update from General Howard in Omaha. "Have heard nothing," the general wired, "from Washington or Chicago."[26]

The capital, as it happened, was nearly deserted. President Cleveland had not been in Washington for a month, having left on

August 7 to attend ex-President Grant's funeral in New York City and then proceeded on to Albany to join his friend and personal physician, Dr. S. B. Ward, for four weeks of hunting and fishing at a secluded lakeside retreat deep in the Adirondack Mountains of northern New York. He could not be reached. In the presidential absence, much of official Washington was likewise out of town, including the secretary of war, the attorney general, and the Chinese minister. The cables from Wyoming had disappeared into a kind of bureaucratic black hole, and only now, late on the afternoon of the fourth, did the government begin to bestir itself.

On the third, Adjutant General Drum, acting head of the War Department in Secretary Endicott's absence, contented himself with forwarding all cables from Wyoming to the secretary at his home in Salem, Massachusetts. Endicott, in turn, instructed Drum to send the cables "to the President, if you know where he is, and consult the Attorney General at once and take such actions as he advises."[27]

"The Attorney General is not here," Drum cabled Endicott on the fourth, "and there are doubts whether I can reach the President."[28] Drum proposed meeting with the secretary of state instead, and the two men conferred for an hour that afternoon. While he was sympathetic to Governor Warren's plight, Secretary Bayard found "a very serious defect" in Warren's cables. According to the Revised Statutes, which the secretary had had examined, troops might be sent to a territory only upon a formal request from the legislature. The governor might request troops only when the legislature was not in session and could not conveniently be convened, and his request must include a statement to that effect. Warren, unaware of the restriction, made no mention of the legislature in any of his cables. Under the circumstances, the best Bayard and Drum could do was to send two companies each to Rock Springs and Evanston, but with orders limiting their duties to preventing "any interruption to the U.S. mails or the routes over which they are received." But the two men were confident, as Drum assured Endicott, that "the mere presence of troops will prevent further trouble and restore order."[29]

It "is all that we can do," Endicott replied, "in the absence of a lawful demand by the Governor."[30]

Warren got the news in Evanston on the evening of the fourth. Troops were on their way, Drum wired, "but before action can be taken for the use of troops to suppress insurrection [you]must first make formal application to the President as indicated in the Constitution and provided for in the Revised Statutes."[31] Warren was astounded;

there was no telling what the rioters would do when they found out about the troops' curious mandate, which they surely would from the next day's papers, if not sooner. He cabled Callaway immediately:

> I am here on ground with no copy of Revised Statutes but considered my dispatch of last night to President sufficient for troops to receive necessary orders. Please oblige me by having Statutes examined legally at once and wire me if any informalities exist. I will correct immediately.
>
> I suggest U.P. make vigorous complaints at Military Headquarters, Omaha, and also to Secretary of War.[32]

Without waiting for a reply, Warren sent an urgent wire to the president: "I earnestly request the aid of United States troops, not only to protect mails and mail routes, but to support civil authorities until order is restored."[33] But he made no mention of the legislature. After sending these cables and reviewing the arrangements for the protection of the Chinese in Evanston, Warren returned to Rock Springs for the night.

SEPTEMBER 5. As Warren suspected, the press had a field day with the latest news from Wyoming. "That the lives of several hundred human beings are in danger at the hands of a mob of fiends makes no difference to the Administration," wrote the man from the Pittsburgh *Telegraph*, "but the mails must be protected."[34]

The Brooklyn *Times* was less restrained—and more representative:

> It is really too bad that the murder of fifty Chinamen in Wyoming should have been regarded by Governor Warren as justifying a requisition upon the President for military assistance to protect human life when the Administration is enjoying its [vacation] in the Adirondacks and elsewhere. It appears that when the requisition was telegraphed to Washington it came into the hands of Adjutant-General Drum [who] hardly knew what to do with it, but finally decided to go and see Bayard. The latter, as Secretary of State, was evidently supposed to have some inscrutable interest in the question whether miners should be allowed to recklessly slaughter Chinamen in Wyoming. The two gentlemen were closeted together for an hour and it was then announced . . . that no action will be taken for the present except to dispatch two companies of troops to Rock Springs

for the purpose of "protecting the United States mails." Hardly an instance is to be cited in the history of Territorial governments in which a formal requisition from the Governor of a Territory has been treated in such a cavalier fashion.[35]

The president, meanwhile, had still not been notified. "It was announced," the *Times* continued, "that the wholesale outrages at Rock Springs were not of sufficient importance to be allowed to trouble the mind of President Cleveland." Thus, while the rest of the country read about the Rock Springs massacre in the newspapers, the president would not learn of it for another two days.

Studying the Salt Lake papers in Rock Springs on the morning of the fifth, Warren discovered the defect in his troop request and wired Washington at once to the effect that the legislature was not in session and could not be convened to provide for the emergency.

Except for an incident involving the Mormons, Rock Springs was quiet on the fifth. The two companies of soldiers, a total of eighty men, arrived just after dawn and began setting up camp. Another delegation met with the governor that morning to assure him, reported the man from the New York *Evening Post*, "that 'everything is now quiet. All the men have gone to work [which was clearly not the case] . . . and as the Chinamen have left we have no further cause for complaint.' The coolness and impudence of the statement took him fairly aback and he merely replied that he hoped everybody would be satisfied in the end."[36]

The mob, meanwhile, was waiting for the outcome of the crisis now looming in Evanston where the situation grew worse every hour and to which Governor Warren hurriedly returned after breakfast.

The mob in Evanston—coal miners, railroad workers, and anyone else with a grievance against the UP, the Chinese, or A. C. Beckwith— read the Salt Lake papers that morning too and knew that the troops which had just arrived were mere window dressing. But they also realized that Warren and the UP would be trying their best to get the troops' orders changed and that the time for decisive action against the Chinese was running out. In the afternoon four hundred people attended a meeting in Downs Hall to review their choices.

There were several other developments on the fifth. Chinese trackmen who worked on section gangs throughout Wyoming and eastern Utah performing routine maintenance on tracks and bridges refused to go to work and demanded passes to Evanston. In that town and Rock Springs, Mormon miners, who had been going to work each day since the massacre, were told that if they continued working, they would be run out of town. The Mormons, who had asked for and been refused passes from the company, stayed home on the fifth, armed themselves, and made preparations to move their families to Salt Lake.

The meeting in Downs Hall broke up in the early evening. Later that night, a number of Evanston's most prominent citizens received letters warning them to stop employing Chinese labor and asking them to use their influence to rid the town of Chinese altogether. A special delegation called personally on A. C. Beckwith to inform him that unless all sojourners were out of Evanston in three days, he would be shot. "They claim to be 500 strong," Callaway told Adams, "and to mean business."[37]

In Boston, the weary Adams was still trying to move the government. His latest appeal, on the night of the fifth, went to Secretary Endicott "as the President is not now in Washington or attending to business."

> A massacre has occurred in Wyoming,[he began]. A large number of laborers and others peaceably engaged in legal vocations have been driven from their work and are not permitted to return to it . . . . Up to this moment the men thus murdered or driven from their work have been Chinamen. The Mormons are now threatened. . . . The civil authorities of Wyoming Territory have officially notified us that they are unable to protect us.
>
> Under these circumstances we find ourselves incapacitated from keeping our track, bridges, and buildings in proper repair; in other words we cannot perform the duties which we were chartered to do. . . . The mere presence of troops known to be under orders not to act except to protect United States property is not sufficient. In view, therefore, of the interests I have in charge, I would most respectfully but most earnestly ask that the government would state what course it intends to pursue.[38]

SEPTEMBER 6, 7. On the morning of the sixth, the white miners at Almy walked off the job and warned the more than four hundred Chinese at that site that anyone who went into the mines would not come out alive. The Chinese held a meeting and decided to move into Chinatown in Evanston. They asked the company for protection and were escorted from Almy by troops. They left their possessions behind after receiving guarantees from the company, but several hours later, the camp was ransacked and partially destroyed. The next day, Callaway closed the Almy mines. Two of the three largest mining camps of the UP system were now out of production.

The arrival of the Almy Chinese raised the number of sojourners jammed into Evanston Chinatown to more than sixteen hundred, virtually the entire Chinese population of Wyoming. On the afternoon of the sixth, a delegation called on Ah Say and urged him to take his people out of the territory. At the same time, in a related move, Governor Warren was presented with a petition signed by 256 citizens of Evanston: "We, the undersigned, know that it is the wish of the Chinese to leave this place as soon as they receive their pay for labor performed by them for their employers. We, therefore, petition his Excellency to use all lawful means to have the said employers pay off their Chinese laborers at once, so they may depart from this place in peace."[39]

The petitioners were telling the truth; by the afternoon of the sixth, most Chinese feared another massacre and were anxious to leave Wyoming. Ah Say, on their behalf, called on Beckwith to ask for the two months' back pay owed most of the Chinese, but Beckwith, after conferring with UP officials, refused. In essence, the Chinese now became hostages of the UP, hostages the company could not even protect.

Alarmed at the mounting tension, Colonel Anderson, in charge of the two companies in Evanston, wired General Howard for reinforcements and a Gatling gun. In Rock Springs, meanwhile, Colonel Chipman had also requested reinforcements amid rumors that a gang was about to attack the jail in Green River where several suspects arrested in connection with the massacre were in temporary custody.

On the seventh, miners in Evanston asked for a meeting with the governor, Beckwith, and Superintendent Dickinson. The meeting took place at 2:00 P.M. in the governor's private car at the railroad depot. The committee of six miners asked the company not to employ Chinese at Almy again. The superintendent would not promise, but he proposed instead to make Rock Springs or Almy an all-Chinese camp and reserve the other site for whites. This was not what the committee sought, nor could it speak for the men in Rock Springs. The meeting broke up inconclusively.

An hour later, the miners announced that their ultimatum to

Beckwith had now expired—one day early, as it happened—and that the Chinese must leave at once. "The committee," Callaway reported to Adams, is "now on [its] way to notify Beckwith."[40]

"Unless United States Government can find way to relieve us immediately," Warren cabled the President, "I believe worse scenes than those at Rock Springs will follow and all Chinamen be driven from Territory. I beg an early reply and information regarding attitude of the United States Government."[41]

"As the case now attends," Adams wired Secretary Endicott, "a condition of war exists in the Territory."[42]

Grover Cleveland emerged tanned and fit from the north woods on the afternoon of the sixth. "His flesh," the *New York Times* reported, "although not diminished by the exercise of hunting, fishing, and tramping through the woods, seemed solid and firm."[43] The president ate supper at Dr. Ward's home in Albany, then took an overnight train to Washington. He arrived at Union Station at 8:00 A.M. on the seventh and was taken by carriage to the White House.

At the State Department, meanwhile, Secretary Bayard was in a meeting with Cheng Tsao Ju, the Chinese minister, who had just returned to the capital the previous evening. The minister reminded the secretary that by the terms of the Chinese-American Treaty of 1880 and the Burlingame Treaty before that, the U.S. government was committed to the protection of all Chinese citizens residing in the country in the event they met with "ill treatment at the hands of any other person." The massacre in Rock Springs, the Minister respectfully submitted, could be construed as "ill treatment".

From this meeting Bayard went directly to the White House and was in conference with the president until noon. Cleveland decided to postpone any action until the matter could be discussed by the full cabinet at its next regularly scheduled meeting the following morning.

In the afternoon, Adjutant-General Drum received a wire from General Schofield at division headquarters in Chicago. "I suggest," the general advised, "that protection be extended to the property and employees of the company, including those engaged in providing the necessary fuel for the service of the road."[44] Drum informed the president, who had just received Warren's latest cable, and Cleveland, without waiting for the cabinet meeting, approved the change of orders.

The following morning, September 8, six days after the massacre, General Schofield wired Governor Warren: "I am authorized by the

President to use United States troops in case of actual necessity to protect the lives and property of Chinese laborers in Wyoming and to aid the civil authorities in preserving the peace. I have given the necessary orders."[45]

Thus, for the first time in its history, the U.S. government, under a treaty with a foreign power, employed its armed forces to maintain domestic order. Warren, always correct, wired Drum and asked him to thank the president for his "prompt assistance."[46]

7

Sadder and Wiser

We are going to have a strike on the Union Pacific, probably the largest strike that has yet been seen.
—CHARLES ADAMS, *Letter of September 18, 1885*

The Sixth Infantry, under the command of General McCook, was quartered at Camp Murray, Utah Territory, several hours' march from Wanship Station, the nearest railhead. At 4:30 in the afternoon of September 8, a mounted messenger rode into camp with a telegram for the general. He was to take six companies and proceed at once to Wanship, whence his men would board special troop trains sent by the Union Pacific, bound for Evanston and Rock Springs, Wyoming Territory. The soldiers arrived at the railhead late in the evening and left for Wyoming just after midnight. Shortly before dawn on the ninth, two companies disembarked at Evanston, and the other four proceeded to Rock Springs. There were now a total of ten companies of the United States Army, over five hundred soldiers, at the scene of the recent disturbances. The mobs in both towns, bowing to the military's superior strength, dispersed, and civil authorities resumed control. One week after the riot and massacre in Rock Springs, the crisis in southwestern Wyoming was over.

Sheriff Young began immediately to make arrests. Though between 100 and 150 people participated in the riot in full view of the entire community, almost no one was willing to cooperate in identifying suspects, either from sympathy with the rioters or fear of reprisals. In the end, Sheriff Young made only sixteen arrests, beginning with Isaiah Whitehouse and William Jenkins, in whose rooms the trouble

Federal troops on duty in Rock Springs, 1885. (Photograph from The Sweetwater County Historical Museum, Green River, Wyoming)

first started. Most of the suspects were young men, ten of them married, and all but three or four were coal miners. One who was not was Richard Keenan, a gambler from Laramie, the man who shot the Chinese laundryman Ah Lee.

The accused were taken to the county jail in Green River where a reporter visited them soon after and found them "laughing and singing and not at all uneasy as to the results":

> Their incarceration was apparently a matter of form, and as the sheriff took them up the street he did not have to watch to see that none ran away, but allowed them to refresh themselves at the beer saloons and then proceeded to the bastille where they were locked in without protest. There will be little trouble . . . the men being willing to answer for what they have done, and the unanimous opinion of the people sustaining them in their course.
>
> It is doubtful if they will be released on bail, but if the bail is fixed

at any reasonable figure there is $100,000 ready to be put up for them. Able counsel will be retained. . . . It is not believed that any jury will be found in the Territory which will convict the prisoners [or] that a single point in the indictment will be made to stick.[1]

The prisoners appeared before the county judge the morning after their arrest and were formally charged with riot, arson, murder, and robbery. Once a grand jury could be empaneled, the judge explained, the accused and any witnesses that could be found would have to appear to answer questions, and if the jury found sufficient evidence of wrongdoing, the prisoners would have to stand trial. Though bail was not normally allowed for such serious offenses, the judge made an exception, and all sixteen suspects, upon paying $500, were released the following day. They hired a prominent Laramie lawyer to represent them (paid for by the Knights of Labor) and returned to Rock Springs free men. "Any attempted trial or punishment of the men who murdered the Chinese," General McCook predicted, "will prove a burlesque and farce."[2]

Meanwhile, other "evidence" was being compiled for the grand jurors at the coroner's office in Rock Springs where an official inquest into the causes and circumstances of death was convened each time a

Chinese delegation sent to investigate the massacre. General McCook is at far right. (Photograph from The Sweetwater County Historical Museum, Green River, Wyoming)

new corpse was brought in from Chinatown. The physician-chairman of these inquests was none other than Dr. Murray, the man seen riding his horse up and down the streets of Chinatown at the height of the massacre, shouting, "No quarter." In each instance, the inquest was over in a matter of minutes, the jurors satisfied with the finding that "the deceased came to his death from gunshot wounds [or fire], the cause of same being unknown to us."[3]

"For my part," one of the jurors, a local butcher, later confessed to a visiting reporter, "I couldn't say nothing else. We supply the Chinamen as well as the Americans with meat, and as I thought the Chinamen might come back, we fixed the verdict . . . and of course we didn't want to know what Americans did it, though we knew all the time."[4]

"The conduct of the coroner who investigated the causes of death seems strange to me," the Chinese minister subsequently wrote Secretary Bayard, "but with my imperfect knowledge of American procedure I prefer not to criticise it."[5]

In all, twenty-five bodies were eventually recovered. They were laid in pine coffins and buried near Chinatown, feet pointing toward the Celestial Kingdom. Another twenty-six sojourners, missing since the day of the massacre, were never seen again. The final death toll was put at fifty-one, the highest ever for a race riot in American history.

Meanwhile, Charles Adams wanted his coal mines back, and he was anxious on another score as well: to demonstrate to the miners in Rock Springs and to workers all along the line that the railroad, not union activists, made company policy. He agreed completely with Isaac Bromley, his personal assistant, who wrote him on this subject a few weeks later from Washington Territory, that: "whatever else may be doubtful, one thing is very certain to my mind, and that is that within a very short time the Company must come to a hand-to-hand encounter with its own employees and settle the question whether the Company or the Knights of Labor shall control and run the road."[6]

In this particular respect, the first week of September was turning out to be one of the worst on record for America's railroads. The expulsion of the Chinese and the closing of UP mines in Wyoming was serious enough, but it was followed by an even greater setback: the loss of the Wabash strike, officially settled on September 3, one day after the riot in Rock Springs.

Trouble on the Wabash had begun back in June when members of the order called a wildcat strike on the home turf of the Wabash in Missouri. In less than six weeks, the strike spread to three other lines in three other states, and by the end of July, had become the largest action ever undertaken by the order. The issues were fundamental: The strikers demanded an end to discrimination against members of the order and the railroad's formal recognition of an employee's right to join a labor union.

In the middle of August, union representatives, led by Joseph Buchanan, gathered in St. Louis for a meeting with A. A. Talmadge, general manager of the Wabash. But Talmadge slipped away hours before the meeting was to begin and headed for New York to consult with his mentor, Jay Gould. Finally reached by wire, Talmadge declared there was no trouble on the Wabash and no need to meet with the Knights. Buchanan, in the most sweeping directive ever issued by the order, then called on all Knights on all lines, including the UP, not to handle any Wabash stock and threatened to call further strikes against any line that tried to force its employees to defy this instruction.

Buchanan and his colleagues followed Talmadge to New York and insisted on a meeting. Gould encouraged Talmadge to give in. Though he was no longer in charge of the UP, Gould still held controlling interest in a number of other railroads and was not eager to see the strike spread. The two sides met in Gould's office on the twenty-sixth, and Buchanan presented the union's demands. Talmadge asked for a week to consider, promising to give his answer at a meeting in St. Louis on September 30. Terence Powderly himself, the head of the order, went to that meeting—and accepted Talmadge's congratulations. The Knights had won. "No such victory," the St. Louis *Chronicle* declared that evening, "has ever before been secured in this or any other country."[7]

As the first challenge to a major railroad in the post-Wabash era, the Rock Springs affair would be watched closely by both sides. However Adams and Callaway might have preferred to handle the situation in Wyoming, circumstances demanded the strongest possible show of force. In the event there was no contradiction: "The one thing that would seem to me irretrievable," Adams wrote Callaway, "would be that we should show any signs of weakness."[8]

This stand categorically ruled out any suggestion of negotiating with the miners. Already, on the eighth, Adams had ordered Callaway not to meet with a grievance committee that had asked to see him. "These men represent felons," he wired. "We cannot deal with them in any way until order is restored. Our grievances with those whom this committee represent are infinitely greater than any grievances they can ever represent against us. Exercise great discretion, but be perfectly firm."[9]

In the circumstances there was only one course of action open to the company: the Chinese would have to be brought back to Rock Springs. Adams was not blind to the probable consequences: a miners' strike at the very least, most likely in all ten company coal camps, and quite possibly a more general strike by the Knights of Labor. In fact, Adams relished the prospect of provoking the order into a strike. "Such an opportunity as the Rock Springs massacre," he wrote Callaway, outlining his strategy, "is not likely to offer itself again. I shall be greatly disappointed . . . unless this matter is brought to a head. . . . If the Knights of Labor [can] be compelled to stand before the country with their organization in direct alliance with murderers, desperadoes and robbers it would be worth to us almost anything."[10]

On the morning of September nine, half an hour after the reinforcements from Camp Murray arrived, several hundred Chinese were marched under armed guard from the Evanston Chinatown to the railroad depot and onto a train of twenty-two boxcars. When they asked where they were being taken, they were told San Francisco. After the Chinese were loaded, a special car bearing Governor Warren and UP officials was brought up and coupled to the back of the train. The caravan left Evanston shortly after 10:00 A.M. "Two-hundred and fifty soldiers and six-hundred and six Chinamen now on their way to Rock Springs," Callaway wired Boston. "Will arrive there tonight."[11]

"It was in the darkness of night," wrote a reporter from New York, "when our train reached the scene of the late, atrocious riot. Before we drew up at the station we were lighted by the camp fires of the troops quartered near the line of the road. As the train stopped it was in the midst of a crowd of hooting miners who were cursing Governor Warren, Beckwith, Quinn and Co., the soldiers and the government."[12]

The train was directed onto a siding just west of where Hong Kong had stood, and a grisly scene presented itself as the sojourners descended from the boxcars. "When we arrived there," they wrote in their affidavit to the Chinese minister,

> we saw only a burnt tract of ground to mark the site of our former habitations. Some of the dead bodies had been buried by the company, while others, mangled and decomposed, were strewn on the ground and were being eaten by dogs and hogs. Some of the bodies were not found until they were dug out of the ruins of the buildings. Some had been burned beyond recognition. It was a sad and painful sight to see

the son crying for the father, the brother for the brother, the uncle for the nephew, and friend for friend.[13]

Scores of Chinese began digging beneath the ruins of their homes to look for money they had hastily buried before their flight. By late evening, they had recovered over $12,000.

The next morning, company carpenters were up early marking off building lots while workmen unloaded construction materials enough for sixty cabins. The new Chinatown was intended to have a total of seventy houses, ten to be shipped in from Twin Creeks, Utah, the rest to be built on the spot. The houses, twelve feet by twenty, designed to hold ten workers, would be erected in rows separated by broad streets.

Army crews were also out marking off lots that morning. The troops—there were now more soldiers in Rock Springs than coal miners—were to be housed in permanent accommodations at what came to be known as Camp Pilot Butte. Two large double houses were to be built for officers and a twenty-foot-long barracks for enlisted men. The message of all the frenzied building was not lost on the group of miners who gathered to watch: the Chinese—and the army—had come to stay.

Any lingering doubts about the company's position were dispelled the following day when D. O. Clark, superintendent of the Union Pacific Coal Company, arrived from Omaha to supervise personally the reopening of the Rock Springs coalfields. Clark's first act was to fire forty-five miners suspected of participating in the riot, and his second was to announce that the mines in Rock Springs would officially reopen the next morning. Angry colliers threatened to derail trains and tear up tracks, but Clark ignored them. "The mutineers scowl, but they do not meet together to talk or drink. Were it possible for them to make further trouble, this silence might be ominous. But they are completely cowed."[14]

The miners cabled the order in Denver to ask for advice and support.

The cable posed a serious dilemma for the union. The return of the Chinese was a direct challenge to organized labor; the order could pass and concede a round to the company, or it could take up the cause of the Rock Springs colliers. The difficulty was that while their cause was as legitimate as ever, the miners had disgraced themselves by their behavior. For the order to plead the miners' case without appearing to condone their actions would require the utmost dexterity, and even

The Chinese lived in boxcars when they were brought back after the massacre. (Photograph from The Sweetwater County Historical Museum, Green River, Wyoming)

then, most of the subtleties of the whole affair would no doubt be lost on the general public. But the temptation was strong; for the first time in a decade, the mines at Rock Springs were closed. If they could be kept closed long enough, the UP would be forced, at long last, to talk to its coal miners.

The responsibility for the Rock Springs affair fell to Thomas Neasham, one of Buchanan's deputies and the man who had first organized the miners in Wyoming (mainly Carbon) and Montana the previous autumn. Neasham was an ambitious, self-serving Scot with a fondness for strikes. Isaac Bromley, who knew him, called Neasham "a pestilential demagogue,"[15] and Adams, who had met him once in Denver and pronounced him "an inflated ass,"[16] was in fact counting on Neasham to play into the company's hands. "Unless I wholly mistake that man," he told Callaway, "he is not difficult to deal with. He is hotheaded, impulsive, Scotch. Nothing he has said or done leaves upon me the impression that he is strong. He is simply active. Under the circumstances, my disposition would be to give him rope. With a little handling and direction, he could be the most useful tool we have."[17]

But Neasham proceeded with caution. He preferred to have the miners try to work out the matter locally by themselves; only when all other schemes were exhausted could the intervention of the order be justified. He cabled some advice and words of encouragement, and waited to see what would happen next.

The attempted reopening of the Rock Springs coalfield on September 12 was a failure. Less than a quarter of the Chinese could be persuaded to report to the mines, even with a military escort, and these were quickly scared off by threats and jeers from white men who had gathered at each pit entrance. The following day, the scene was repeated. "Things are not moving at all well," Coal Superintendent Clark cabled Callaway. "The Chinese are so easily frightened. . . . When they start to go toward the mines a guard of white miners meets them and scares them back. Our mine bosses that have charge of the inside work leave the mines when Chinese go in and engineers leave

Camp Pilot Butte. (Photograph from The Sweetwater County Historical Museum, Green River, Wyoming)

the engines when we start to pull out Chinese coal. I don't know as I will be able to get any men to work at all."[18]

Clark was troubled by the rumors that the soldiers had no stomach for their mission. "They curse the duty which compels them to sustain the alien against the American," the Rock Springs *Independent* reported,[19] and Clark took the report seriously. "I fear the military are inclined to go the way of all Wyomingites in this matter," he wrote Callaway. "I am trying to get some of Pinkerton's men out here to protect the property of the company. I don't like at all the way things look here."[20]

By the third day, the Chinese had had enough. Angry at being tricked into returning to Rock Springs in the first place and now newly afraid for their safety, the sojourners wanted to leave. "By this time," they wrote of their condition that week, "most of the Chinese have abandoned their desire of resuming their mining work, but inasmuch as the riot left them each with only the one or two articles of clothing they have on their persons, and as they have not a single cent in their pockets, it is a difficult matter for them to make any change in their location. Although protected by Government troops, their sleep is disturbed by frightful dreams and they cannot obtain peaceful rest."[21]

A committee of Chinese approached UP officials to ask for passes to California, but the company refused. Hoping to buy their way out, the Chinese then appealed to A. C. Beckwith for the back wages they were owed, but Beckwith, as he had done in Evanston, said no. In desperation, the sojourners even approached members of the order to ask for ticket money. The astonished Knights suggested a strike instead, and the following day, the Chinese stayed home.

"We are rapidly running out of coal with which to operate the road," Callaway notified Adams on the fourteenth, "Almy and Rock Springs mines practically closed now. Have been unable as yet to get men to go to work at Rock Springs. I understand they have been getting considerable encouragement from Denver and that Engineers at mines will decline to go to work when ready to start up. Feeling against the Company seems to be intense all along line."[22]

"We clearly cannot yield in this matter," Adams replied, "and submit to the Knights of Labor. It would be better for us to close permanently. It is therefore a mere question of coal supply. What arrangements can you make to procure coal from other quarters?"[23]

Callaway was buying coal wherever he could find it—from the Central Pacific, from mines in Iowa and Missouri, and from Bishop Sharp in Salt Lake City. In the meantime, he was also trying to reopen the mines at Almy. He asked Isaac Bromley, Adams's personal assistant whom the president had sent west to investigate the Rock Springs affair, to approach Beckwith about the possibility of starting up with Chinese, but it was Beckwith's "feeling," Bromley reported, "that if such an order was given he would not give a nickel for his life and should take the first train out of town."[24] Callaway dropped the idea and decided instead to open Almy as an all-white camp, with as many Mormons as he could find.

As the standoff dragged on, the miners, on Neasham's advice, asked again for a meeting with Callaway to present their grievances. Adams, though he did not intend to negotiate, did not want the company to appear unreasonable and advised Callaway to comply. Initially the miners' committee intended to go to Omaha, but Callaway suggested the men present their case to Bromley, who was already in Rock Springs, and a meeting was arranged for the fifteenth. The day before, Neasham went to Wyoming to help the miners prepare their case.

The meeting began at 11:30 A.M. in Bromley's private car near the depot. Bromley, Superintendent Dickinson, and D. O. Clark represented the company, and the miners' brief was argued by Dr. Murray, committee chairman, Isaiah Whitehouse, and Neasham. Bromley described the encounter in a report to Adams:

> The inquiry had hardly begun before Mr. Neasham appeared in the capacity of a sort of counsel for the committee. During the whole hearing he constantly interrupted witnesses, putting words in their mouths . . . and in every way acted the part of a sympathizer with and defender of the rioters.
>
> After I had permitted the committee to go on for some time, I attempted to get at the facts connected with the outbreak. . . . When I asked [Whitehouse] if he could give me some information as to what occurred between himself and the Chinamen, he answered at once and positively that he would not. Not only that, but he interrupted every person questionned upon the same point and told them not to answer. . . .
>
> It is hardly necessary for me to comment upon [the testimony] any more than to say that the method of presentation, the substance of the complaints and the general character of the proceedings [should] convince any fair-minded person that all the grievances and complaints were an after-thought, that the outbreak having occurred, everyone who had, or ever supposed himself to have, any cause of complaint had been called upon to rack his memory and

bring forward his grievance in justification of what had been done.[25]

After the meeting, which left both sides further apart than ever—
"the information I have received astounds me," Neasham told the
press[26]—the committee made another attempt at reconciliation in a
private meeting with Clark and Bromley. The miners proposed that
the company reinstate all white men, including those Clark had fired,
and dismiss all Chinese until an investigation could be conducted and
anyone found guilty of participation in the massacre could be identified
and punished. "I told them I could not entertain their proposition,"
Clark wrote Callaway later that evening, "as the Chinese were here to
go to work."[27]

Clark was doing his best to reopen the mines. He refused passes
to Mormon miners asking to leave, and on the sixteenth he went to Salt
Lake to meet with Bishop Sharp and make arrangements to hire
experienced Mormon engineers. He then returned to Rock Springs to
deal with the Chinese, who, though they may have been in Rock
Springs "to go to work," were in fact on strike. Clark directed Beckwith
to close his store and cut off all supplies to the sojourners, and
threatened in addition to turn any Chinese who would not cooperate
out of the boxcars where they were staying until their homes were
completed. After a day, the Chinese called off their walkout and
agreed to return to the mines, though some sixty managed to leave,
forty by train and twenty on foot. "This great and glorious government,"
wrote one Wyoming editor, "is using bayonets and gatling guns to
establish a slave market labor system in Wyoming. Rock Springs will
become a Chinatown. It might be well to rename it in accordance.
Beckwith,Quinn and Co. would not be inappropriate."[28]

Clark then announced that UP mines in Rock Springs would now
officially reopen on Monday morning, September 21.

With negotiations broken off and the company showing increasing
signs of being able to resume operations, the pressure on Neasham to
call a strike was mounting. And it would have to be a general strike,
for if the company was able to get coal out after Monday, then only a
strike that included operating men—engineers, conductors, brakemen,
and firemen—would meet the case. Chinese colliers could dig all the
coal they pleased, but with the operating men out, there would be no
way to move it. To pull off a general strike, however, was not such an
easy matter; twice during the past year the order had tried to get the
operating men to go out in support of striking miners, and both times
they had refused. The only hope for a general strike, and this was by

no means guaranteed, was total participation at the local level—if all the miners in Rock Springs were out, in other words, and all the operating men too. If engineers in Denver and Omaha were going to be asked to strike, then engineers in Rock Springs had better be out.

Neasham met with the miners' committee on the evening of the fifteenth and promised he would call a general strike on the colliers' behalf and that he would put strike funds at their disposal. He spent all day on the sixteenth laying the groundwork with other groups in Rock Springs, then returned to Denver, leaving "instructions." Callaway wired Adams, "that no white men should go to work until further notice from Denver. I don't mean to force a fight," Callaway continued, "But it seems to me we should dismiss every man who obeys this order. I have asked the Government Directors for their judgement. Will you kindly let me have yours?"[29]

A fight, of course, was precisely what Adams hoped for, a fact he thought he had made painfully clear: "We here think you too timid. The point suggested does not admit of a moment's consideration. You must crowd the fighting. This is what we want. Dismiss every man who stops work on orders from Denver. In case of general strike at any mine, close the mine and do not open it until you get orders from here."[30]

Over the weekend, tension mounted as both sides braced for Monday's confrontation. On Saturday, Clark distributed two notices to all company employees. The first was a copy of a cable sent to him by Callaway: "This company desires to resume the operation of its coal mines at Rock Springs at the earliest possible moment. You will be good enough to notify all concerned that such of the miners and other employees who have not been dismissed can have work at their places upon Monday morning next. All persons not then at work will be paid off and notice given that they must not again be employed in any capacity in the service of this company."[31]

The second notice was from Clark himself: "Notice is hereby given that work will be resumed in mines No. 1, 3, 4, and 5 on Monday morning, Sept. 21st at seven o'clock. All miners and other employees are expected to return to their places at that time, with the assurance that they will receive while at work and at their homes such protection from the civil and military authorities as will insure their personal safety."[32]

As the UP stepped up the pressure, miners suspected of wavering were visited by members of the order and told to support the strike or be out of town by Sunday night. "Two miners waved their hands at me to come and speak to them," a collier named Dunn later testified, "I went down the walk with them, and they asked me how I would like to be ordered out of town in twenty-four hours. Says I, 'What for?' He says, 'You are not a workingman, and you are of no use in this camp.' I said, 'I am getting sick of the whole affair, and do not care how soon I go.' He says, 'In twenty-four hours.' I took him for a very sober man."[33]

A mysterious fire broke out near Archer on Sunday, destroying half a mile of track and snowsheds. Adams told Callaway to take special precautions to protect the pay car: "We do not want to supply the strikers with funds."[34] Sheriff Young appointed a number of special deputies, and the company brought in a contingent of Pinkertons to help guard railroad property. Both the deputies and the special agents were threatened by the miners and told to leave.

The government directors passed through over the weekend on their annual inspection tour of the road and were alarmed enough at the situation to send an urgent cable to the secretary of the interior: "We find such a condition of affairs as in our opinion endangers the property of the road, jeopardizes the interest of the government and calls for prompt interference."[35]

Governor Warren weighed in with his support as well: "Allow me to express an earnest wish," he cabled Callaway, "that your road will under no circumstances recede in the slightest degree from the stand taken that Chinese shall work and criminals shall not."[36]

The other side was ably represented by most of the region's newspapers. "While it is the duty of the government to suppress insurrection and rebellion," observed the Omaha *Herald*,

> it becomes a serious question whether the army is to be employed as a police at the dictates of a corporation which was mainly instrumental in causing the outbreak. The slave drivers in the south, in their palmiest days, never presumed the army should be employed as a posse to be placed over their chattels and keep them from mutiny.[37]

> Boss Callaway and his aides in Omaha are determined to trample the Western man under their feet [opined the Laramie *Daily Boomerang*]. It is a shame that they can bulldoze the people of a territory like this. The quicker Adams, Callaway and the rest are fired, the better it will be for the country.[38]

Back in Boston, Adams waited for the storm to break. "We deem it merely necessary," he told Callaway in a final pep talk, "to repeat that the most unyielding firmness is expected from you. No concessions of any description are to be made."[39] In the meantime, in a letter to his friend E. L. Godkin, the editor of the New York *Evening Post*, he confided his thoughts on the eve of what he expected, and hoped, would be "the largest strike that has yet been seen":

> I think that a general strike all over the Union Pacific on the part of the so-called Knights of Labor is going to take place within a few days. I no longer want to see it put off. I want to have it and have it now. It should be distinctly understood that ... whatever they may say, the largest labor organization in the country is going to strike in order to secure to murderers and robbers peaceful and undisturbed enjoyment of their violence. They will, of course, endeavor to work up a long list of alleged wrong, but at bottom it is just what I say. ...
>
> I call your attention to the matter now because I want you to be ready to give a direction to public opinion. I do not believe that this country is yet ready, in spite of demagogues and sophistry, to sustain a strike ordered in aid of a band of assassins.[40]

On September 21, nineteen days after the riot and massacre, the Rock Springs coalfield officially reopened. A military guard called for the Chinese at their boxcar village and escorted them to work. A few whites threw stones, and one sojourner had his face slapped and his hat stolen by a group of six white women, but there were no other incidents. No white miners, including pit bosses and surface men, reported for work, nor did the carpenters building the army barracks and the new Chinatown. Miners at Almy and Grass Creek also honored the strike call, but operating men did not. Production for the day was 10 percent of normal.

Meanwhile, Neasham cabled the order's terms to Callaway: "We respectfully submit that to adequately meet the case the removal of the Chinese from the system, and the removal of Beckwith, Quinn and Co. and D. O. Clark from authority is required. Nothing else will suffice."[41]

For the next ten days, the balance in the struggle tilted back and forth, neither side the clear winner. On Tuesday, all six mines were back in operation, and twice as many Chinese reported for work. On Wednesday, Clark, who had gone to Salt Lake to confer with Bishop Sharp again, returned to Rock Springs with twenty-five Mormon pit bosses. But, as Clark wrote Callaway from the Mormon capital, getting labor to fill some of the predominantly white occupations such as pit boss and engineer wasn't hard; the problem was keeping them: "If we get some men at work, someone whispers to them that they had better quit. Very few threats are used, but the request is usually enough. The day before I left we hired six men. The next morning none of them were on hand. It has been this we have had to contend with."[42]

Clark pulled out more stops. At midweek, he dismissed twenty strikers and announced that on Saturday the company's offer of travel passes to fired strikers would expire and that on Sunday any UP employee not back at his job would be turned out of company housing.

Throughout the week, Neasham traveled the line in search of a general strike. On Tuesday night, he addressed a mass meeting of Knights in Omaha ("a great harangue was made," Callaway reported, "principally confined to abuse of the United States").[43] On Wednesday, he was in Carbon looking for solidarity, on Saturday back in Rock Springs urging the miners to stand firm. "Neasham and his crowd are apparently moving heaven and earth to get a [general] strike," Callaway informed Adams. "D. O. Clark says white miners don't propose to leave Rock Springs. The Knights of Labor have undoubtedly undertaken to see the miners through. Very few of them have left."[44]

For a few hours on the morning of October 1, the strike seemed about to come alive when the men at UP mines in Carbon and in Louisville, Colorado, joined the walkout. But there was hardly time to toast the victory when more sobering news arrived: Eighty men from the Grass Creek mines, also on strike since the twenty-first, showed up as scabs in Rock Springs, and the men at Almy returned to work. Four days later, the rest of the men at Grass Creek went back.

The loss of Carbon hurt—the mines there and in Louisville were immediately closed—but Callaway was optimistic; with Almy back in operation and production at Rock Springs approaching one-third of normal, he foresaw "no coal famine." The only danger now, he told Adams, was that the union might "convince our trainmen to decline to handle the coal, which will brings matters to a head."[45]

"This," a frustrated Adams shot back, "is exactly what we wish."[46]

The miners' cause, jolted by the breaches in solidarity, received another blow later that same week when grand-jury proceedings against those accused of the massacre opened in Green River and degenerated almost at once into the burlesque and farce everyone had predicted. To begin with, there was the composition of the jury: Eleven of the sixteen members were from Rock Springs, including the ubiquitous Dr. Murray, and several were coal miners. The judge himself, it was widely rumored, belonged to the Knights of Labor. The court had tried to appoint a more objective jury, but anyone not known to be in sympathy with the accused was afraid to sit. "I was told to report for jury duty in Green River," David Thomas recounted, "and when D. O. Clark asked me why I did not wish to serve I replied that I did not feel that my back was bullet proof."[47] General McCook remarked that the only way a fair trial could be obtained was to declare martial law in Sweetwater County, the murderers to be arrested and tried by a military commission.

The jury heard the testimony of thirty-three individuals—bullies patrolled in front of the courthouse to discourage unfriendly witnesses—not one of whom was Chinese. But this wasn't for the Chinese consul's lack of trying. "I told the U.S. District Attorney General," Colonel Bee explained to a reporter in California, "that if he could guarantee proper protection, I would furnish him Chinese witnesses who could identify every white engaged in the assault. He said he would attend to the matter and let me know. He then went off to Evanston and I have never seen or heard from him since. . . . You must remember that these Chinese and whites have been working together for the last eight years and are a trifle more than familiar with each other's countenances."[48]

At a preliminary pretrial hearing, the question of Chinese testimony was raised, and the judge ruled that the Chinese were "unworthy witnesses."

Only one snippet of testimony ever leaked out to the public, and it was promptly picked up and reprinted in newspapers across the country. The question, to the Reverend Timothy Thirloway, was How, in his opinion, did the fires in Chinatown start? In other words, was the charge of arson appropriate? The reverend thought not: "I stepped out of my house with my wife and saw the first two houses that were set fire. . . . Four Chinamen came out a short distance from us. They had hardly left when we saw the buildings on fire. I am quite convinced that they were fired by the Chinamen."[49]

"The Reverend Timothy must be amazed at his own moderation," remarked the editor of *The Nation*. "It was quite open to him to charge the Chinese with suicide, or with murdering each other, or driving each other into that awful region where they died of starvation or as the wild beast's prey."[50]

"If the cause of the miners requires such misrepresentation as this to gain sympathy and support," noted the editor of the Rock Springs *Independent*, a strong supporter of the colliers, "it must be a very weak cause indeed."[51]

The jury's verdict was a foregone conclusion:

> We have diligently inquired into the occurrences at Rock Springs on the second day of September last, and though we have examined a large number of witnesses, no one has been able to testify to a single criminal act committed by any known person on that day. . . . Therefore, while we deeply regret the circumstances, we are wholly unable to return indictments.
>
> We have also inquired into the causes that lead to the outbreak at Rock Springs. While we find no excuses for the crimes committed, there appears to be no doubt abuses existed there that should have been promptly adjusted by the railroad company and its officers. If this had been done, the fair name of our Territory would not have been stained by the events of the 2nd of September.[52]

Cheering broke out in the courtroom when the verdict was read, and the acquitted, after a victory feast in Green River, returned to a heroes' welcome in Rock Springs.

Neasham's general strike eluded him at every turn; the appalling lack of solidarity among the miners; the "ghastly mockery of justice," to use President Cleveland's phrase, just concluded in Green River; and several well-publicized declarations by Adams, Callaway, and the government directors that the company would turn the line over to the government before negotiating with the order—these factors kept the wary operating men on their guard and a good safe distance from the coal strike. Already the men in Carbon, on strike only two weeks, regretted their action, and a number tried to leave to look for work in Almy. On two successive evenings in mid-October, they piled their belongings on wagons and proceeded to the railroad depot where they were turned back by hardliners and their tools and household effects were dumped on the ground. Sheriff Rankin deputized twenty Pinkertons to help keep the peace.

The miners in Rock Springs, tired of Neasham's promises, wrote directly to Terence Powderly, head of the union, asking for "a direct reply to the following question: Are the Knights of Labor, as an organization, coming to our relief or are they not?"[53] Powderly wrote back that this was the first he had heard that the order was involved in the affair and wanted to know all the particulars before making any decision.

While Powderly educated himself and Neasham went off to plead the miners' case in Hamilton, Ontario, where the order was holding its annual convention, production at Rock Springs was

*The new Chinatown. (Photograph from The Sweetwater
County Historical Museum, Green River, Wyoming)*

increasing daily, to nearly two-thirds of normal by the last week of
October. There were thirty white surface men at work, with another
forty Mormons expected any day, and over seven hundred Chinese,
more sojourners than before the massacre. The new Chinatown would
be finished in two weeks, housing for the military in another month.
Some ninety miners had left, including all those accused of the riot
except for delegate-elect Whitehouse, while another one hundred
colliers, too poor to relocate, clung to the wreckage of their walkout.

By the second week in November, it was over. Neasham, disposed
now in any case to admit defeat, received a sharp rebuke from
Powderly. "This Chinese mess in Wyoming has gone far enough," the
Grand Master Workman wrote, "and any thought of a strike on this
matter is entirely out of the question."[54] Neasham notified the men in
Carbon and Rock Springs, and directed his secretary to draft a letter
to Callaway on the miners' behalf. "These men now see their mistake,"
the letter began. "We would ask you to . . . consider the circumstances
connected with the trouble and allow such men as remain to resume
work."[55]

The company, on Callaway's orders, was magnanimous in victory.
Miners in Carbon were rehired on November 12, and a number of men
in Rock Springs were also put back on the payroll. Louisville, operating
at a loss even before the strike, was never reopened, and Almy became
an all-white camp. "Mr. Neasham is going to allow us to manage the

property in our own way for the present," Callaway wrote Adams. "He is finding out that the unfrequented road to immortality is somewhat thorny. I think he goes home sadder and wiser than he came."[56]

But Adams, his general strike evaporating before his eyes, was not to be consoled: "It was a glorious time to have struck the organization straight from the shoulder and between the eyes," he answered. "We will never have such another chance."[57]

8

Remedial Measures

I am compelled to bring to the immediate attention of your excellency the deplorable and defenseless condition of many thousands of my countrymen resident in the States and Territories of the Union adjacent to the Pacific Ocean.

—CHENG TSAO JU, Chinese Minister
to Secretary of State Bayard

As coal miners and the Union Pacific clashed in southwestern Wyoming, the fire from Rock Springs spread across the West, igniting a series of anti-Chinese explosions the length and breadth of the Rockies. Because of the failure of the Exclusion Act of 1882 to contain Chinese immigration, conditions on the coast had grown steadily worse and anti-Chinese sentiment steadily deeper. And yet, as Congress and the president had taken up (and in their view, solved) the Chinese question, there was little interest in or support for further action. It seemed now that only a crisis could break the impasse and provoke Congress to revisit the issue.

And so it was that the Rock Springs massacre, "precipitating," in the words of one historian, "the most violent and sustained period of anti-Chinese outbursts in the history of the United States,"[1] jolted the nation into renewed awareness of the Chinese question and brought about its ultimate resolution. Indeed, so great was the explosion from the Bitter Creek incident that before the excitement was over, mobs rose against the sojourner in eight Western states, the army was repeatedly called out, the president again obliged to intervene, Americans were threatened in China, Congress was forced to enact sweeping reforms, and the presidential election campaign of 1888 had a divisive new issue. Inevitably, the furor engulfed the UP, forcing the company to reexamine its Chinese strategy and in the end to abandon it. The company may have just won the battle for Rock Springs, but it was about to lose the war for Chinese labor.

California erupted first, in almost every locality. The worst trouble was at Eureka, where hundreds of Chinese were rounded up, robbed, run out of town, their homes burned. In all, the Chinese were driven out of more than twenty-five communities around the state, most of them fleeing to San Francisco, where they were soon joined by thousands of other refugees from towns and cities across the West.

In Santa Cruz, New Mexico, the Chinese were given twenty-four hours to leave. Near Douglas Island, Alaska, one hundred sojourners were herded onto a boat and set adrift in the Pacific. In Grass Creek, Utah, all Chinese were run out by the end of September. On the night of September 21, the day the mines reopened in Rock Springs, the Knights of Labor called a mass meeting in Butte, Montana, site of extensive copper mines and a flourishing Chinatown, and the assembled throng, mostly miners, passed a unanimous resolution calling for the dismissal of all Chinese labor and its complete expulsion from the territory no later than October 1.

There was trouble in Idaho too, in the mining camp at Orofino where there was a small Chinese community, including a store run by the merchant Lee Kee Nan. For some time, white miners had been complaining about Lee because he refused to sell them goods on credit. On the night of September 3, a local white restaurant owner was found murdered. A week later, three white men, acting with no legal authority, seized five sojourners, including Lee, and locked them up in the town jail. Ten men guarded the premises, denying the Chinese access to legal counsel or a hearing. Three days later, an escort arrived to take the Chinese to the courthouse for a trial. Instead, the Chinese were marched to a place three miles outside of town and hung.

There was more trouble in Wyoming as well. In Laramie, a special deputy was appointed to watch over the Chinese. One week after the massacre, members of the order in Cheyenne announced a boycott of all businesses employing sojourners, and the head of the order paid a call on the editor of the *Leader* to warn him that unless his paper changed its antilabor tone, he would be run out of town. On the eighteenth posters appeared all over the capital, warning that any Chinese found in Cheyenne after October 1 would receive "a coat of tar and feathers [and be] run from the city on a rail."[2] By the twenty-ninth, half of the Chinese in Cheyenne had left for California.

There was trouble even in Washington, D.C., in Congress's own backyard, where the Women's Industrial League was holding its annual convention. "For the good of the public and the health of the country," the women resolved, "the Chinese laundries must go." The women lashed out at Secretary Manning for allowing the Treasury Department's towels to be washed at local Chinese establishments, and the embarrassed secretary was obliged to make new arrangements. A week later, three weeks after the massacre, the Chinese question was still on the agenda when the president met with his cabinet.

The worst violence to erupt in the wake of the Bitter Creek massacre occurred in the Pacific Northwest, especially in Washington Territory. The disturbance began as a series of isolated incidents but quickly spread into a concerted systematic movement to drive the Chinese out of the entire region. The story was the same as elsewhere in the West; hard times, more workers than work, the Chinese keeping to themselves, (and keeping their money to themselves), a dash of racism, newspapers hungry for good copy, and the inevitable union agitation. Bromley, Adams's assistant from Boston who had gone into the region after completing his investigations in Wyoming, reported on the mood to his chief: "The news of the Rock Springs massacre reached Washington Territory at a time when there was great public indignation at the non-enforcement of the Exclusion Act and the organized evasion of its requirements. It needed only this to set loose the lawless, hoodlum element on the Chinese."[3]

Violence first broke out on September 7, five days after the massacre, at a hop farm in Squak Valley, King County. Thirty-five Chinese hop pickers had just bedded down for the night when they were suddenly set upon by a mob of white men and two Indians. Three Chinese were killed in the melee, the rest driven out, their tents looted and burned. The next day, the Celestials left for the coast. Though seven men were eventually arrested, anti-Chinese feeling in the region was so high that no witnesses appeared to testify, and the accused were released. "The Chinese massacre in Wyoming was cowardly enough," noted the *Daily Alta* in condemning the lawlessness, "but that in Squak Valley has made it seem an exhibition of chivalrous courage."[4]

Within two weeks, armed masked men carried out similar raids against Chinese miners at the Coal Creek and Black Diamond coal camps. In both cases, public sentiment had already forced the mine owners to dismiss the Chinese; the raids just speeded up their exodus. The Chinese were eventually picked up by special trains and taken to Seattle.

As fleeing Chinese from throughout the region descended upon

Seattle, a call went out from the Knights of Labor for a conference, known as the Puget Sound Congress, to consider means of expelling the Chinese from the territory. Each town, labor organization, and labor union was instructed to elect three delegates. The congress met in Seattle on September 28: "Every socialist and anarchist who could walk or steal a ride was a self-elected but nevertheless welcome delegate," complained one newspaper.[5]

The congress, chaired by Mayor Weisbach of Tacoma, passed two important resolutions: All citizens were asked to "discharge all Chinese in their employ immediately," and the delegates were empowered to convene meetings in their hometowns for the purpose of electing "ouster committees" to oversee the departure of the Chinese by no later than November 1.[6] The committees would then have until November 6 to report any irregularities.

The day after the congress adjourned, several hundred Chinese were dismissed from mines in Seattle and the vicinity. Four carloads were taken to Portland where they were met by a large demonstration organized by the Knights, and the rest were absorbed into the Seattle Chinatown. A few nights later, Seattle met to elect its ouster committee. That same evening, a ticket-holders-only meeting was held in Frye's Opera House where the prominent citizens of the city, reconciled to the sojourner's departure, met to discuss how the exodus could be managed more peacefully. At the end of the meeting, Sheriff McGraw divided the city into districts and secretly appointed deputy sheriffs and district captains to be responsible for the safety of the Chinese in the event of violence.

On October 10, the Seattle ouster committee passed through Chinatown to notify its occupants of the November 1 deadline and paid warning calls at the same time at the homes of citizens who employed Chinese. Several days later, the mayor of Seattle, who had organized the meeting at the opera house, received an anonymous letter advising him to "go slow . . . and let the China biz alone." The letter also told him of "a cache of dynamite within one mile of Seattle ready to be utilized anytime after November 1st."[7] One week before the deadline, anti-Chinese forces sponsored a mass torchlight parade through downtown Seattle, attended by some twenty-five hundred demonstrators from across the territory: "The Seattle Chinaphobes were joined by six-hundred enthusiasts from Tacoma, New Castle, Renton, Black Diamond and McAllister. . . . Three bands played during the march and the paraders carried numerous transparencies. Typical banners read: 'Discharge your Chinamen;' 'White laundries are good enough;' 'Down with the Mongolian slave;' 'Get off the fence; either for or against.' On nearly all could be seen 'John, Go.' "[8]

As the first neared, the Chinese consul in San Francisco appealed to Governor Squire to make arrangements to protect the Chinese and to contact federal authorities if necessary. Governor Squire assured the consul that he was ready to meet any contingency.

The first came and went without incident, but serious trouble in nearby Tacoma on the third brought matters to a head. Led by Mayor Weisbach himself, Tacoma's ouster committee and some five hundred friends armed with clubs and rifles invaded the Chinese quarter and demanded the immediate departure of its residents. Wagons were brought up, and the mob did the sojourner's packing for him. The entire population of Chinatown, some three hundred, was then escorted to the depot and bundled onto a waiting train. A few Chinese who resisted were seized and thrown bodily into the cars.

The train pulled out of the station and proceeded out of town in the direction of Portland. Eight miles down the track, the train suddenly came to a halt and the Chinese were ordered off. Here a second mob, armed and mounted, herded the Chinese together and marched them a mile into the wilderness. "If any looked back or walked slowly, whips were used to hasten their speed, no rest being given even to those who were sick."[9] Those who had not been robbed before were robbed now, and the whole band—famished, cold and penniless— was abandoned just as darkness fell and a thunderstorm broke. A few who had managed to conceal some money bought their way to Portland during the night, and the next day the Chinese community there collected enough funds to send a train back to Tacoma to rescue their stranded countrymen.

News of the "Tacoma solution" electrified Seattle and precipitated a crisis. The order announced a mass rally for the evening of the fifth, and that afternoon three representatives from the union sat down with five prominent Chinese bosses and the Seattle citizens' committee to ask for the peaceful speedy departure of the Chinese. The committee of prominent citizens heard the labor leaders out, then advised the Chinese that if they stayed, there was no guarantee they or their property could be protected. The Chinese agreed to leave as soon as possible, asking only for enough time to pack and dispose of their property.

The mood in the city and across the territory was tense and ugly. The Chinese, fearing a spontaneous outbreak, appealed to Governor Squire for protection. The governor issued a proclamation to all citizens of Washington, warning them to refrain from acts of violence and to "array yourselves on the side of the law. If you do not . . . you have only to look to the step beyond; which is simply the fate of Wyoming and the speedy interference of U.S. troops."[10] General Sheridan, following the situation from the War Department, wired General Pope, in command of the Pacific division, to stay "informed and alert" lest the Washington disturbances spread down the coast.[11] In the meantime, the revenue cutter *Walcott* was ordered into Seattle harbor, where it lay at anchor with its guns unsheathed.

The union rally on the night of the fifth was bitter and boisterous, eventually degenerating into a shouting match. No serious business could be conducted, so a second meeting was called for the night of the seventh. In the interim, over 150 Chinese fled the city. On the seventh, Governor Squire called in the army; two companies of the Fourteenth Infantry left Fort Vancouver after lunch and arrived in Seattle just past midnight. That same afternoon, President Cleveland issued an order to the citizens of Washington Territory: "I do hereby command and warn all insurgents and persons who have assembled at any point within the Territory for the wrongful purpose [of expelling the Chinese] to desist therefrom and disperse and retire peaceably to their respective abodes on or before 12 o'clock meridian on the 8th of November."[12]

The next day, the city was quiet.

With troops to guarantee their safety, the remaining Chinese elected to stay in Seattle. The city seethed quietly for three months while members of the ouster committee went on trial and the anti-Chinese lobby tried to push restrictive laws through the territorial legislature. Throughout the region, sentiment against the sojourner, though muted, grew steadily.

The explosion came during the second half of January when in the same week the legislature voted against several strong anti-Chinese bills and a jury acquitted those accused of conspiring to drive the Chinese from Seattle. With the troops no longer on the scene, these two developments—that legal attempts to expel the sojourner were a dead end and that illegal attempts were hard to prosecute—seemed like an invitation to the anti-Chinese forces to finish the job they had started in November.

On Saturday evening, February 6, a giant anti-Chinese rally was held at the Bijou Theatre in Seattle. Acting quickly before the authorities could raise the alarm, those present organized a number of committees to be sent into Chinatown the following morning to rouse the Chinese and herd them down to the port where a steamer would be waiting to take them to San Francisco. The action was to commence at daybreak and be completed by one o'clock.

At dawn on the seventh, the hit squads, led by the chief of police, descended on the Chinese quarter, burst in on the sleeping Chinese, loaded their belongings on wagons, and marched the startled sojourners through an immense crowd to the port. By 10:30 A.M. some 350 Chinese, virtually their entire community, stood huddled under armed guard on the wharf while the *Queen of the Pacific* made ready to receive them. Governor Squire, who happened to be in Seattle on business, was briefed on the situation and immediately cabled the secretary of war for troops. He also issued a proclamation calling for an end to the lawbreaking. "This was read to the crowd [and] was received with a howl of defiance."[13]

As tension mounted, a snag developed on the docks. Captain Alexander was happy to take the Chinese away, but it would cost $7 a head, and none of the Chinese had any money. Lest the crowd try to force the ship, the captain ordered his crew to break out their hot-water hoses. A committee was then formed to take up a collection, and by 1:30 P.M., enough money had been raised to buy one hundred tickets, but just as the *Queen* was about to pull away from the dock, a messenger passed through the crowd and handed the captain a writ; the presence of all one hundred of his passengers was required in court. A quick-thinking Chinese merchant, it turned out, had sworn out a writ of habeas corpus, charging that his countrymen were being illegally held on the ship.

The Chinese spent the night in a warehouse on the wharf. The next morning, the one hundred ticket holders were escorted by deputy sheriffs through an angry crowd to the courthouse where Judge Greene informed them that they had a legal right to remain in Seattle and that the government would do all it could to protect them. In his personal opinion, the judge went on, the Chinese would be better off if they left. All but sixteen sojourners took the judge's advice.

After the hearing, the Chinese were marched back to the dock and onto the waiting steamer. By now, enough money had been collected to buy tickets for all the Chinese, but Captain Alexander could accept only 196 passengers, his legal limit. After a hasty conference, it was announced that the remaining Chinese would sail on the next steamer, one week hence. At 11:30 A.M., the *Queen of the Pacific* set sail for San Francisco.

The deputy sheriffs and the Seattle Home Guard now tried to march the remaining 150 Chinese back to Chinatown. The streets were thronged with angry demonstrators, shouting threats and trying to manhandle the Chinese. As one group of rioters tried to break through, the Guard suddenly opened fire, and five men fell:

> The crowd recoiled several paces, horror-struck. At once the Seattle
> Rifles, who were just leaving the dock, came up on the double quick
> and formed a line to support the Home Guard.... The scene for a time
> was remarkable. The troops formed a hollow square facing up and
> down Commercial and Main streets. The Chinamen in their midst
> had thrown their blanket rolls on the ground at the first fire and were
> crouching behind them. Outside the square a tremendous crowd
> swayed to and fro with cries of rage and defiance.[14]

The impasse dragged on for a full hour until the crowd finally parted enough to allow the escort to proceed. Later that day, the governor declared martial law, suspended habeas corpus, announced a curfew, and cabled the president for immediate assistance.

Federal troops returned to Seattle the following day, but this time only forty Chinese decided to stay on in the city. Five days later, the steamship *Elder* took the rest of the sojourners to San Francisco. "The trouble is over," wrote a local reporter, "and the people have proved their ability to govern themselves. They have done this not as the friends of the Chinese, but as the friends of law."[15]

All across the West, the story in broad outline was the same as the Chinese were driven out of community after community to make their way to a dubious safety-in-numbers on the coast. Those who could afford it bought passage back to China. Some twenty thousand left in 1885, another eighteen thousand in 1886, more than in any other two-year period. Several hundred others took trains east to look for work in Cincinatti and Pittsburgh. But the average sojourner, robbed as he was driven out, his property confiscated or burned, had no means of altering his situation. The strain on the port cities, meanwhile, such as Seattle, Portland, and especially San Francisco, became unbearable. "At the present time the condition of our countrymen on this coast is deplorable in the extreme," the president of the Six Companies wrote the Chinese minister that winter: "There are over one-hundred thousand Chinese who have no place of safety in which to dwell, and many millions of dollars of property have no protection. Our people are absolutely terrorized and are flocking to San Francisco where great destitution exists among them. Absolutely no protection is afforded [us] by the governor of this state or the sheriffs of the various counties. Our suffering is inexpressible."[16]

Cheng Tsao Ju, the able, eloquent Chinese minister to the United States, made an urgent appeal to Secretary of State Bayard, and through him to the president, for the government of the United States to stand by its treaty obligations and assume responsibility for protecting the Chinese. "I am compelled," he wrote Bayard,

> to bring to the immediate attention of your excellency the deplorable and defenseless condition of many thousands of my countrymen resident in the States and Territories of the Union adjacent to the Pacific Ocean... and I deem it my duty to appeal for the adoption of such prompt and vigorous measures as will secure to my persecuted and outraged countrymen the protection to their lives, their homes, and their property which is guaranteed to them by the solemn treaties between the two Governments.
>
> I purposely refrain from giving the details of the [outrages] as I deem them of too revolting and sickening a character to be repeated in this note, and I am too well-acquainted with the noble and humane sentiments which inspire your excellency to think that such a statement is necessary to awaken your sympathy and indignation.[17]

Cheng then went on to spell out his government's demands; "that the persons guilty of this murder, robbery and arson be brought to punishment, that the Chinese subjects be fully indemnified for all losses... and that suitable measures be adopted to protect the Chinese residents in Wyoming Territory and elsewhere in the United States from similar attacks."

Other appeals also descended on the administration in the wake of the Rock Springs affair, most notably from the anti-Chinese lobby, riding the wave of violence and civil disorder to new heights of power and now counting among its supporters virtually every important segment of society on the coast and every politician who cherished his job. Some voices, like Governor Warren's, pushed for stricter enforcement of the Restriction Act, but for most Westerners, the act was a dead end, "full of ambiguities and omissions,"[18] which more rigid enforcement would do nothing to correct. Only new legislation would meet the case. Scores of memorials and petitions poured into Washington from around the country, urging Congress to pass tough new restrictions, and a number of bills were taken up by a variety of committees in both houses.

As the pressure mounted, there was alarming news from China: Letters and cables describing the Rock Springs massacre and subsequent events on the coast were being posted on walls in Canton, and natives of the Celestial Kingdom were threatening reprisals against Americans living in China. On March 16, the American consul in Shanghai wrote the American minister in Peking that he could no longer guarantee the safety of U.S. citizens in Hong Kong and Canton province and was requesting military protection. Minister Denby protested to the Chinese government, dispatched a gunboat, and cabled the secretary of state for further instructions. "If Chinamen are driven out and outraged here," the Chinese consul in New York noted in an interview that week, "why can't our people drive out all Americans from China?"[19]

At the height of the crisis, Cheng Tsao Ju received new instructions from his government. He was directed to inform the secretary of state that if the United States did not move at once to condemn the Rock Springs massacre and indemnify its victims, China "would immediately proceed to collect the indemnity from American citizens in business in the Imperial Territory and withdraw its protection."[20]

The plight of the threatened Americans in Canton caught Grover Cleveland's attention in a way the plight of the Chinese in the West never seemed to. On March 2, in the same week the gunboat was dispatched to Hong Kong, Cleveland sent a special message to Congress in direct reponse to the demands of the Chinese government. In it, the president publicly deplored "the shocking occurrences at Rock Springs . . . and the still more recent outbreak in Washington Territory" and declared, in something of an understatement, that "the condition of the Chinese . . . in the Western States and Territories is far from being satisfactory." In consequence he decreed that "all the power of this Government should be exerted to maintain the amplest good faith toward China in the treatment of [its people], and the inflexible sternness of the law in bringing wrongdoers to justice must be insisted upon."[21] And he urged Congress, in a carefully worded passage, to approve new legislation:

> Whilst the U.S. Government is under no obligation to indemnify these Chinese subjects, . . . in view of the palpable and discreditable failure of the authorities of Wyoming to bring justice to the guilty parties and considering further the absence of provocation on the part of the victims, the Executive may be induced to bring the matter to the benevolent consideration of Congress, in order that that body, in its high discretion, may direct the bounty of the government in aid of innocent and peaceful strangers whose maltreatment has brought discredit upon the country; with the distinct understanding that such action is in no wise to be held as a precedent, is wholly

gratuitous, and is resorted to in a spirit of pure generosity toward those who are otherwise helpless.[22]

The indemnity provision, in the amount of $147,748.74, was eventually passed and the money distributed to the claimants, but few of the victims of the countless other incidents that occurred in the aftermath of the Rock Springs riot were ever compensated, nor did the law, in the president's words, prove particularly "stern" in bringing wrongdoers to justice. But the two measures technically met the demands of the government of China and effectively defused the crisis in Canton.

Cleveland may have had his eye on Americans in China, but his mind was on Americans at home. He was in the middle of a closely fought presidential election campaign that summer, and he was determined to appropriate the China issue for the Democrats. Anti-Chinese legislation won votes not only in the three states along the Pacific slope but among workingmen everywhere. The second part of the president's special message to Congress was directed squarely at the anti-Chinese lobby: "The admitted right of a Government to prevent the influx of elements hostile to its internal peace and security may not be questioned. . . . If existing laws are inadequate to compass the end in view, I shall be prepared to give earnest consideration to any further remedial measures, within treaty limits, which the wisdom of Congress may devise."[23]

Congressional wisdom, in short order, devised a bill with four major provisions: No Chinese laborer could immigrate to the United States for the next twenty years. No laborer already in the country who left for any reason could return unless he had a wife, child, parent, or a debt exceeding $1000 in America. No Chinese holding valid work certificates issued under the Restriction Act of 1882 would be allowed in the country if they should happen to be away when the new act took effect. Certificates for the exempt classes of nonlaborers must now bear a photograph.

The bill eventually passed both houses of Congress and was signed by Cleveland on August 24, 1888. Before it could become law, however, the bill, which was in the form of a series of proposed revisions to the Sino-American Treaty of 1880, had to be approved by the governments of both parties. Ten days after Cleveland signed the legislation, a press dispatch from London reported that the Chinese government had refused to sign the agreement, taking particular exception to the provision that prevented the return of laborers who happened to be outside the country when the new treaty took effect. Due to the dangerous mood on the coast, there were some twenty thousand laborers in that particular category, more than one-sixth of all the Chinese in the country.

The Democrats, in an unseemly rush to get the act on the books before the election and forestall any presidential embarrassment (it was the Republicans who precipitated the present crisis by adding the controversial provision during the floor debate), immediately introduced an extraordinary measure that would make the new legislation the law of the land with or without China's approval of the treaty revisions. The author of the measure was one William L. Scott, Cleveland's campaign manager. "For decency's sake," several senators urged tabling the bill at least until the press report could be verified and China's rumored objections received and studied. But partisan politics prevailed, and the measure passed both houses on September 21 and went to the president. By coincidence, China's objections arrived on Cleveland's desk the same day, but the president ignored them and signed the bill into law.

"I was not prepared to learn," the astonished—but always correct—Chinese minister protested to Secretary Bayard, "that it is the practice of governments to act on newspaper reports . . . [or] that there was a way recognized in the law . . . whereby your country could release itself from treaty obligations without consultation or the consent of the other party."[24]

While the storm raged without, Rock Springs was quiet. In the months following the massacre, operations returned to normal, and coal production increased. The statistics, from the UP's point of view, were very encouraging: On August 30, two days before the riot, there were 331 Chinese and 150 whites in the Rock Springs coalfield, and total production for the day was 1,450 tons; on November 30, two months later, there were 532 Chinese and 85 whites at work, and production was 1,610 tons. The new Chinatown, meanwhile, was completed and occupied by mid-November, and the army barracks were ready at the end of the month. From all outward appearances, the victory of the UP over the Knights of Labor was complete.

It was also quite hollow, for in fact the days of the company's Chinese strategy were almost over. Not even the mighty Union Pacific, it turned out, could resist the forces unleashed across the West in the wake of the Bitter Creek massacre. While there had never been any support for the Chinese policy outside the upper echelons of the company, the outcry over the past decade had always been fitful, uncoordinated, and largely confined to company employees and labor organizations. After the events in Rock Springs, the outcry was unanimous from all sectors of society, and congressional action was imminent. For the UP to defy its own employees and the Knights of Labor was one thing; to defy universal public sentiment was quite another. Adams and Callaway moved to set the railroad's house in order themselves before they were forced to by others.

As early as September 25, only three weeks after the riot, the scale of public reaction was already clear. "In considering the Chinese question," Bromley wrote Adams that day from Portland where he had just completed his tour of the line,

> it is to be taken into account that the universal sentiment along the line of the road is anti-Chinese. The Company cannot defy public opinion or undertake an organized defense of Chinese labor. It must accept results, however illogically reached, [and] among these results is the fact that public opinion on the Chinese question has been formally expressed in the Exclusion Act. It would not be wise to fly in the face of it by undertaking to replace white labor on any large scale, in the mines or elsewhere, by Chinese.[25]

Adams concurred in the assessment: "The odium in which this company is held is a heavy burden to us," he wrote Callaway several weeks later.

> Confidentially, I have very little doubt in my mind that, in view of the prevailing public sentiment which you describe throughout the whole country west of the Missouri as well as Wyoming, we shall have to give up Chinese labor to a great extent. You cannot operate a railroad successfully in the face of an all pervading public sentiment, no matter how wrong it may be. If you do you are then making your railroad a machine for propagating ideas. Railroads are commercial enterprises, they are not humanitarian, philanthropic or political.[26]

While bowing to the inevitable, the company was careful to insist on its complete innocence in the Rock Springs affair and to deny any responsibility for what transpired there. "The massacre was without cause or excuse," was the railroad's official position, as stated by the government directors in their report on the incident, "unless a violent and widespread race prejudice may furnish the latter."[27] Bromley, in an interview published in the Cheyenne *Daily Leader*, said the massacre was completely unexpected: "It broke out," he said, "like lightning from a clear blue sky."[28] And Adams, answering a massive petition sent to the company on behalf of white workingmen all along the line, used the occasion to insist again on the railroad's blamelessness: "The Union Pacific Railway Company is a corporation chartered by the National Government," he wrote. "As such its directors do not feel that it is within their province to discriminate against any persons of any nationality, color, or sect."[29]

That said, the company proceeded to dismantle ten years of labor policy. Adams began by decreeing that Chinese railroad workers, most of them members of section gangs, should gradually be replaced by whites. Regarding miners, he vetoed Callaway's plan to reopen Almy as an all-Chinese camp and also quashed Callaway's alternative proposal for the several hundred Almy Chinese (to move them to Rock Springs), saying the scheme smacked of "unnecessary bravado."[30] Instead the sojourners were paid off and sent back to San Francisco, where they arrived the first week of October and immediately booked passage for China.

The Chinese were to be phased out of Rock Springs as well, though over a much longer period of time, more than fifteen years, and in a way that afforded small comfort to the white miners. Mormons, of course, were to take up the slack wherever possible, and where it wasn't, cutting machines, just then making their appearance in the coalfields, were to be used. "I take it for granted," Adams wrote Callaway on October 6, "that we look to the use of improved machinery for our escape from the existing dilemma. . . . That has got to supplant both the striking white labor and the condemned Chinese labor."[31]

As early as September 17, four days before the mines at Rock Springs reopened, Coal Superintendent Clark had raised the possibility of trying machines, and by the twenty-first a representative of a cutting-machine company was already in town studying the possibilities. "These machines," noted the editor of the *Daily Boomerang*, "will be just the kind of labor wanted. [They] don't smoke opium, have the leprosy, ask for more wages, go on strikes or join unions."[32]

After a two-month trial, Clark reported that the machines were working "very nicely and I think will save at least 20 cents in every ton of coal. One machine will replace at least 33 miners." The only problem, in fact, was what to do with the excess Chinese, "as we will not want over half of them."[33]

Adams was delighted. "Beginning with Rock Springs," he wrote Callaway in January, in one of his last references to the situation there,

"I hope that machines will be quietly slid in until the miners have to slide out, and when I say out, I mean not only out of the mines, but out of Wyoming."[34] The UP may have finally lost the struggle for Chinese labor, but the white coal miners had certainly not won it.

Nor could the Knights of Labor help them. Less than a year after the massacre, at the height of its power and influence, the order suddenly collapsed. In the end, the union was the victim of its own remarkable success and in particular its phenomenal growth, which betrayed its members and leaders alike into a false sense of the order's actual strength, leading them into one ill-advised action after another and culminating in the disastrous Southwest strike of 1886 against their old nemesis, Jay Gould. By an unfortunate coincidence, the day the order lost the Southwest strike was the same day a bomb went off at a union-sponsored rally at the Haymarket in Chicago, killing seven policemen. The two incidents seriously undermined the union's power and appeal, and "by August [1886] the Knights of Labor as an organization had practically ceased to exist on the Missouri Pacific system and was dying out rapidly on all the western railroads."[35] Later in that same year, the nation's colliers abandoned the order and formed their own National Federation.

On his own, Isaiah Whitehouse, the miner in whose room the fight that led to the massacre started, did what little he could to ease the lot of fellow colliers. As the representative from Sweetwater County to the territorial legislature, he introduced a bill to require mine owners to credit miners with the weight of their coal before the slack was removed, but the measure, passed by the general assembly, was vetoed by Governor Warren. And another of Whitehouse's efforts, a bill to outlaw the practice of withdrawing a miner's wages to cover unpaid bills, was also rejected.

Under the circumstances, tension between whites and Chinese in Rock Springs remained high, and although the presence of federal troops in the town was a constant embarrassment to the territory— every week or two, Governor Warren cabled the officer-in-charge in Rock Springs to ask if troops were still necessary—there could be no question of removing them. On one occasion several years after the riot, old Ah Say, still the patriarch of Chinatown, heard a rumor that the government was thinking of withdrawing the army and immediately sent a petition to the secretary of war. "A large number of the perpetrators of [the massacre] still reside in the town," the document read in part, "and are still indisposed toward your petitioners." If his excellency ever contemplated a pullout, Ah Say went on, he must be sure to warn the Chinese well in advance "so that they may make preparation for removal to a place of safety."[36] The troops stayed in Rock Springs for thirteen years, until the eve of the Spanish-American War. Their barracks, one section of which was later incorporated into a wing of a new elementary school, are the sole remaining physical evidence of the Chinese massacre.

The Rock Springs massacre is a curiously unsatisfying story. In the end there are no unabashed heroes, no one to enthusiastically root for. While one sympathizes and may even identify with the miners to a point, their brutality must forever leave a bad taste. The Chinese, whose tragic fate is unpardonable, nevertheless knew—by their own admission—the risks they took in playing the spoiler. And the actions of the UP, whatever one may think of their philosophy, were by turns petty, loutish, and cruel. Only Francis Warren, a man of courage and principle, comes out of this sorry episode with his dignity intact. (Indeed, he went on to become the son-in-law of General John G. Pershing, the richest man in Wyoming and one of the most powerful U.S. senators in the country.)

If there were no heroes in the Rock Springs debacle, there were decided winners and losers. The UP, nominally victorious, never again hired Chinese labor with the same impunity and, in any case, hired fewer and fewer over the years. For their part, thousands of Chinese fled back to the Celestial Kingdom, and immigration fell dramatically. The Rock Springs colliers were also losers, not so much to the Chinese but to the march of progress, embodied in the onset of the era of mechanized coal mining. The winners were the wage earners along the Pacific slope, who for a time found competition more open and employers more respectful of the power of organized labor.

Rock Springs today has changed very little. It is still something of a frontier town and still a mining center. The UP goes through (freight trains only), there is a working mine in Blairtown and there are ten Chinese families. Hong Kong is gone, but you can get a decent meal at the Hong Kong House. The centennial of the massacre was observed several years ago, but most residents are not aware of the history their town made that September afternoon in 1885. As Richard Leow, who works in Lew's Family Restaurant, put it recently: "That's a long time ago."

NOTES

INTRODUCTION

1. Rock Springs *Miner*, September 30, 1950.
2. Arlen Ray Wilson, "The Rock Springs Wyoming Chinese Massacre, 1885," Master's thesis, University of Wyoming, Laramie, 1967.

PROLOGUE

Epigraph is from Mary Coolidge, *Chinese Immigration* (New York: Henry Holt, 1909), p. 41.
1. Charles Wollenburg, ed., *Ethnic Conflict in California History* (Los Angeles: Tinnon-Brown, 1970), p. 68.
2. B. L. Sung, *The Story of the Chinese in America* (New York: Collier Books, 1971), p. 10.
3. *Daily Alta* (California), c. June 1852.
4. Coolidge, p. 22.
5. *Daily Alta* (California), May 12, 1852.
6. *Daily Alta*, May 12, 1852.
7. Coolidge, p. 22.
8. Coolidge, p. 23.

CHAPTER ONE

Epigraph is from Mary Coolidge, *Chinese Immigration* (New York: Henry Holt, 1909), p. 87.
1. Oscar Lewis, *The Big Four* (New York: Alfred A. Knopf, 1938), p. 62.
2. Jack Chen, *The Chinese of America* (San Francisco: Harper and Row, 1980), p. 67.
3. Lewis, p. 70.
4. Lewis, p. 71.
5. B. L. Sung, *The Story of the Chinese in America* (New York, Collier Books, 1971), p. 31.
6. Chen, pp. 67–68.
7. Chen, pp. 68–69.
8. Chen, p. 68.
9. Chen, p. 66.
10. Lewis, pp. 72–73.
11. Union Pacific Coal Company, *History of the Union Pacific Coal Mines 1868 to 1940* (Omaha: Colonial Press, 1940; reprint ed. Green River, Wyo.: Sweetwater Co. Hist. Soc., 1977), pp. 20–22.
12. George Kraus, *High Road to Promontory* (Palo Alto, Calif.: American West, 1969), p. 203.
13. Union Pacific Coal Company, p. 27.
14. Elmer C. Sandmeyer, *The Anti-Chinese Movement in California* (Urbana-

Champaign: University of Illinois Press, 1973), p. 65.
15. Sacramento *Record Union*, January 10, 1879.
16. Coolidge, p. 264.
17. Sandmeyer, p. 43.
18. Sandmeyer, p. 47.
19. San Francisco *Bulletin*, October 25, 1871.
20. *New York Times*, October 26, 1871.
21. Cheng-Tsu Wu, *Chink!* (New York: World Publishing, 1972), p. 149.
22. Alexander McLeod, *Pigtails and Gold Dust* (Caldwell, Idaho: Caxton, 1948), p. 198.
23. Sandmeyer, p. 59.
24. Charles Wollenburg, ed., *Ethnic Conflict in California History* (Los Angeles: Tinnon-Brown, 1970) p. 76.
25. Coolidge, p. 109.
26. Cheng-Tsu Wu, pp. 120, 124.
27. Coolidge, p. 168.
28. Salt Lake *Herald*, September 21, 1885.

CHAPTER TWO

Epigraph is from Francis Birkhead Beard, W*yoming: From Territorial Days to the Present* (Chicago: American Hist. Soc., 1933), p. 297.
1. Howard Stansbury, *An Expedition to the Valley of the Great Salt Lake* (Ann Arbor, Mich.: University Microfilms), p. 234.
2. Stansbury, p. 236.
3. C. S. Dietz, *The Developed and Undeveloped Mineral Resources of Wyoming* (Cheyenne: Wyoming Geological Survey, 1929), p. 115.
4. Union Pacific Coal Company, *History of the Union Pacific Coal Mines 1868 to 1940* (Omaha: Colonial Press, 1940; reprint ed. Green River, Wyo.: Sweetwater Co. Hist. Soc., 1977) pp. 11–13.
5. Virginia Cole Trenholm and Maurine Carley, *The Shoshonis: Sentinels of the Rockies* (Norman: University of Oklahoma Press, 1964), p. 110.
6. Trenholm and Carley, p. 110.
7. Grace Raymond Hebard, *Washakie* (Cleveland: Arthur H. Clark , 1930), p. 212.
8. Hebard, p. 53.
9. Hebard, p. 137.
10. O. O. Howard, *Famous Indian Chiefs I Have Known* (New York: The Century Co., 1907), p. 315.
11. Howard, p. 315.
12. Howard, p. 321.
13. Beard, p. 151.
14. Hebard, p. 212.
15. Hebard, pp. 212–13.
16. Beard, p. 169.
17. Grenville Dodge, How We B*uilt the Union Pacific Railway* (Washington: Government Printing Office, 1910), p. 17.
18. Dodge, p. 17.
19. T. A. Larson, *History of Wyoming* (Lincoln: University of Nebraska Press, 1978), p. 11.
20. I. S. Bartlett, ed., *History of Wyoming* (Chicago: S. J. Clarke, 1918), p. 171.
21. Larson, p. 51.
22. Larson, p. 65.
23. Bartlett, p. 171.

24. *Report of the Government Directors of the Union Pacific Railway Company*, 1873 (Senate Executive Document 69, Serial 2336. 49th Cong., 1st sess.; Government Printing Office, 1886), p. 70.
25. Larson, p. 114.
26. Cheyenne *Daily Leader*, June 18, 1873.
27. *Report of the Government Directors*, p. 70.
28. Charles Edgar Ames, *Pioneering the Union Pacific* (New York: Century-Crofts, 1969), p. 413.
29. Stansbury, p. 234.
30. Robert B. Rhode, *Booms and Busts on Bitter Creek: A History of Rock Springs, Wyoming* (Boulder, Colo.: Pruett, 1987), p. 9.
31. Stansbury, p. 235.
32. Cheyenne *Daily Leader*, c. 1877.
33. Mary Lou Pence and Lola Homsher, *The Ghost Towns of Wyoming* (New York: Hastings House, 1956), p. 65.
34. Union Pacific Coal Company, p. 51.
35. Dell Isham, *Rock Springs Massacre 1885* (Ft. Collins, Colo.: privately printed, 1969), p. 3.
36. Larson, p. 195.
37. Larson, p. 62.
38. Larson, p. 54.
39. Charles Kelly, *The Outlaw Trail* (New York: Devin-Adair, 1938), pp. 164–65.
40. Union Pacific Coal Company, pp. 39–40.
41. Union Pacific Coal Company, p. 75.
42. Anita Bartholdi, "Melting Pot of Wyoming" (Senior English thesis, Rock Springs, Wyo., city library), p. 55.
43. Union Pacific Coal Company, pp. 59–60.
44. Union Pacific Coal Company, p. 47.
45. Union Pacific Coal Company, p. 29.
46. Cheyenne *Daily Leader*, c. 1878.
47. Union Pacific Coal Company, p. 49.
48. Larson, p. 202.
49. Allan Nevins, *The Emergence of Modern America* (New York: Macmillan, 1927), p. 290.
50. Lewis L. Gould, *Wyoming: A Political History* (New Haven: Yale University Press, 1968), p. 30.
51. Gould, p. 30.
52. Gould, p. 31.
53. Gould, p.31.
54. Gould, p. 32.
55. Beard, p. 288.
56. Larson, p. 114.

CHAPTER THREE

Epigraph is from Union Pacific Coal Company, *History of the Union Pacific Coal Mines 1868 to 1940* (Omaha: Colonial Press, 1940; reprint ed. Green River, Wyo.: Sweetwater Co. Hist. Soc., 1977), p. 76.
1. Sidney Dillon to Oakes Ames, December 28, 1875, *Records of the Union Pacific Railway Company* (Lincoln: Nebraska State Hist. Soc.).
2. Richard O'Connor, *Gould's Millions* (New York: Doubleday, 1962), p. 13.
3. Julius Grodinsky, *Jay Gould: His Business Career* (Philadelphia: University of Pennsylvania Press, 1957), p. 129.

4. O'Connor, p. 12.
5. Cheyenne *Daily Leader*, November 8, 1875.
6. Union Pacific Coal Company, p. 76.
7. Laramie *Daily Sun*, November 15, 1875.
8. Laramie *Daily Sentinel*, November 13, 1875.
9. Laramie *Daily Sun*, November 17, 1875.
10. Laramie *Daily Sentinel*, November 25, 1875.
11. Laramie *Daily Sentinel*, November 25, 1875.
12. Laramie *Daily Sentinel*, November 25, 1875.
13. Laramie *Daily Sentinel*, November 25, 1875. It is not clear what happened in Carbon. According to some sources, a Chinese camp was also built there, but if it was, it was clearly never used. The strike there appears to have ended at the same time as the strike in Rock Springs, but it is not certain whether miners were fired or reached a settlement with the company.
14. Laramie *Daily Sentinel*, November 25, 1875.
15. UP President Sidney Dillon to Superintendent S. H. H. Clark, November 26, 1875, *UPR Records*.
16. Francis Birkhead Beard, *Wyoming: From Territorial Days to the Present* (Chicago: American Hist. Soc., 1933), p. 289.

CHAPTER FOUR

1. Laramie *Daily Sun*, November 26, 1875.
2. Salt Lake *Daily Tribune*, September 20, 1885.
3. Salt Lake *Daily Tribune*, September 20, 1885.
4. Letter from A. C. Beckwith, source unknown.
5. George Orwell, *The Road to Wigan Pier* (Middlesex, U.K.: Penguin, 1984), pp. 22–26.
6. Orwell, p. 27.
7. Orwell, p. 20.
8. Robert B. Rhode, *Booms and Busts on Bitter Creek: A History of Rock Springs, Wyoming* (Boulder, Colo.: Pruett, 1987), pp. 33–34.
9. Union Pacific Coal Company, *History of the Union Pacific Coal Mines 1868 to 1940*, reprint ed. (Green River, Wyo.: Sweetwater Co. Hist. Soc., 1977), p. 161.
10. Union Pacific Coal Company, p. 162.
11. Orwell, p. 32.
12. Union Pacific Coal Company, p. 233.
13. Orwell, p. 19.
14. Orwell, pp. 29–31.
15. Isaac H. Bromley, *The Chinese Massacre at Rock Springs, Wyoming Territory* (Boston: Franklin Press; Rand, Avery, 1886), p. 22.
16. Bromley, p. 23.
17. Bromley, p. 22.
18. Bromley, p. 23.
19. Salt Lake *Daily Tribune*, September 20, 1885.
20. Bromley, p. 29.
21. Salt Lake *Daily Tribune*, September 20, 1885.
22. *Annals of Wyoming* (Cheyenne: The Wyoming Hist. Soc., date unknown).
23. Wyoming Writers' Project, *Wyoming: A Guide to Its History, Highways, and People* (New York: Oxford University Press, 1941), p. 246.
24. Union Pacific Coal Company, pp. 92–93.
25. U.S. Congress, House, Committee on Foreign Relations *Report No. 2044*. 49th Cong., 1st sess., 1885–1886 (hereafter, *House Report No. 2044*), p. 28.

26. Union Pacific Coal Company, p. 60.
27. Union Pacific Coal Company, p. 58.
28. Bromley, pp. 85–86.
29. Laramie *Daily Sun*, November 26, 1875.
30. T. A. Larson, *History of Wyoming* (Lincoln: University of Nebraska Press, 1978),
     p. 115.
31. Larson, p. 143.

CHAPTER FIVE

Epigraph is from Isaac H. Bromley, *The Chinese Massacre at Rock Springs, Wyoming
     Territory* (Boston: Franklin Press; Rand, Avery, 1886), p. 55.
1.   Charles Adams to Samuel Callaway, September 1885, *Records of the Union
     Pacific Railway Company* (hereafter, *UPR Records*), (Lincoln: Nebraska State Hist.
     Soc.).
2.   Joseph Buchanan, *The Story of a Labor Agitator* (Westport, Conn.: Greenwood
     Press, 1970), p. 113.
3.   Norman Ware, *The Labor Movement in the United States* (New York: D. Apple-
     ton, 1970), p. xviii.
4.   Ware, p. 134.
5.   D. O. Clark to Thomas Kimball, November 16, 1884, *UPR Records*.
6.   Charles Adams to Sidney Dillon, February 10, 1885, *UPR Records*.
7.   Samuel Callaway to Charles Adams, January 19, 1885, *UPR Records*.
8.   Samuel Callaway to Charles Adams, January 23 & 25, 1885, *UPR Records*.
9.   Anonymous monograph on Charles Adams, Library of Congress, Washington,
     D.C.
10. Charles Adams to Samuel Callaway, January 2 & 29, 1885, *UPR Records*.
11. Samuel Callaway to Charles Adams, January 25, 1885, *UPR Records*.
12. Anonymous monograph on Charles Adams, Library of Congress, Washington,
     D.C.
13. Adams monograph.
14. Adams monograph.
15. Adams monograph.
16. A. J. Poppleton to John Dillon, February 6, 1885, *UPR Records*.
17. Samuel Callaway to Charles Adams, February 7 & 14, 1885, *UPR Records*.
18. Union Pacific Coal Company, *History of the Union Pacific Coal Mines 1868 to
     1940*, reprint ed. (Green River, Wyo.: Sweetwater Co. Hist. Soc., 1977), p. 79.
19. A. C. Beckwith to Terence Powderly, May 5, 1886, Powderly Papers, Letter file:
     April–June 1885, Department of Archives and Manuscripts, Catholic
     University of America, Washington, D.C.
20. Union Pacific Coal Company, p. 80.
21. Bromley, p. 33.
22. *Deseret News* (Salt Lake), September 1885.
23. Bromley, pp. 26, 31.
24. Bromley, pp. 49,54.
25. Bromley, p. 49.
26. *House Report No. 2044*, p. 44 (see chap. 4, note 25).
27. David G. Thomas, "David G. Thomas' Memories of the Chinese Riot," (as told
     to his daughter Mrs. J. H. Goodnough), *Annals of Wyoming* 19, no. 2 (July 1947):
     108.
28. *House Report No. 2044*, p. 30.
29. Rock Springs *Independent*, September 4, 1885.
30. *House Report No. 2044*, p. 30.

31.   *House Report No. 2044*, p. 14.
32.   Rock Springs *Independent*, September 4, 1885.
33.   *House Report No. 2044*, p. 14.
34.   Bromley, p. 55.
35.   The New York *Evening Post*, September 15, 1885.
36.   Bromley, pp. 15–16.
37.   Bromley, p. 79.
38.   *House Report No. 2044*, p. 29.
39.   *House Report No. 2044*, p. 14.
40.   Rock Springs *Independent*, September 4, 1885.
41.   Rock Springs *Independent*, September 4, 1885.
42.   Laramie *Daily Boomerang*, September 6, 1885.
43.   David Thomas, p. 109.
44.   Bromley, p. 50. The Laramie *Boomerang* paints a less flattering picture: Evans
      on his knees pleading for his life.
45.   *Deseret News*, September 4, 1885.
46.   David Thomas, p. 109.
47.   David Thomas, p. 109.
48.   Laramie *Daily Boomerang*, September 3, 1885.
49.   *Deseret News*, September 4, 1885.

CHAPTER SIX

Epigraph is from "Special Report of the Governor of Wyoming to the Secretary of
      the Interior concerning Chinese Labor Troubles, 1885," (hereafter, Warren
      Report), p. 1231.
1.   Joseph Young to Francis E. Warren, September 2, 1885, Warren Report, p. 1231.
2.   Francis Warren to B. A. Downen, February 28, 1890, F. E. Warren Papers,
      Letterbook 4-7-1890 to 11-15-1894 (hereafter, Warren Papers), University of
      Wyoming Archives, Laramie, Wyo.
3.   Thomas Kimball to Francis Warren, Warren Report, p. 1225.
4.   Samuel Breck to Francis Warren, September 3, 1885, Warren Report, p. 1227.
5.   F. E. Warren to President Cleveland, September 3, 1885, Warren Report,
      p. 1227.
6.   F. E. Warren to President Cleveland, September 3, 1885, Warren Report,
      p. 1227.
7.   F. E. Warren to President Cleveland, September 3, 1885, Warren Report,
      p. 1228.
8.   Francis Warren to B. A. Downen, August 28, 1890, Warren Papers.
9.   Francis Warren to Samuel Callaway, September 21,1885, Warren Papers.
10.   Francis Warren to Charles Adams, September 29, 1885, Warren Papers.
11.   Cheyenne *Democratic Leader*, September 17, 1885.
12.   New York *Evening Post*, September 15, 1885.
13.   *Rocky Mountain Daily News*, September 14, 1885.
14.   Laramie *Daily Boomerang*, September 4, 1885.
15.   Samuel Callaway to Charles Adams, September 3, 1885, *Records of the Union
      Pacific Railroad Company* (hereafter, *UPR Records*), (Lincoln: Nebraska State
      Hist. Soc.).
16.   Warren Report, p. 1228.
17.   Warren Report, p. 1228.
18.   Isaac H. Bromley, *The Chinese Massacre at Rock Springs, Wyoming Territory*
      (Boston: Franklin Press; Rand, Avery, 1886), p. 52.
19.   Francis Warren to General O. O. Howard, September 4, 1885, Warren Report,
      pp. 1228–29.

20. Bromley, p. 53.
21. Bromley, pp. 82–83.
22. Charles Adams to Samuel Callaway, September 17, 1885, *UPR Records.*
23. Samuel Callaway to Charles Adams, September 4, 1885, *UPR Records.*
24. Charles Adams to Samuel Callaway, September 4, 1885, *UPR Records.*
25. Samuel Callaway to Charles Adams, September 4, 1885, *UPR Records.*.
26. Warren Report, p. 1229.
27. Secretary of War Endicott to Adjutant General R. C. Drum, September 3, 1885, Adjutant General's Office Files for 1885 (hereafter, AGO Files), National Archives, Washington, D.C.
28. Drum to Endicott, September 4, 1885, AGO Files.
29. Drum to Endicott, September 4, 1885, AGO Files.
30. Endicott to Drum, September 5, 1885, AGO Files.
31. Drum to Francis Warren, September 4, 1885, AGO Files.
32. Francis Warren to Samuel Callaway, September 4, 1885, Warren Papers.
33. Francis Warren to President Cleveland, September 4, 1885, Warren Report, p. 1229.
34. Pittsburgh *Telegraph*, September 5, 1885.
35. Brooklyn *Times*, September 5, 1885.
36. New York *Evening Post*, September 15, 1885.
37. Samuel Callaway to Charles Adams, September 5, 1885, *UPR Records.*
38. Charles Adams to Endicott, September 5, 1885, AGO Files.
39. *Rocky Mountain Daily News*, September 15, 1885.
40. Samuel Callaway to Charles Adams, September 7, 1885, *UPR Records.*
41. Francis Warren to President Cleveland, September 7, 1885, Warren Report.
42. Charles Adams to Endicott, September 7, 1885, AGO Files.
43. *New York Times*, September 6, 1885.
44. General Schofield to Drum, September 7, 1885, AGO Files.
45. Schofield to Francis Warren, September 8, 1885, Warren Report, p. 1231.
46. Francis Warren to Drum, September 8, 1885, Warren Report, p. 1231.

CHAPTER SEVEN

Epigraph is from Charles Adams to E. L. Godkin, September 18, 1885, *Records of the Union Pacific Railway Company* (hereafter, *UPR Records*), (Lincoln: Nebraska State Hist. Soc.).
1. Isaac H. Bromley, *The Chinese Massacre at Rock Springs, Wyoming Territory* (Boston: Franklin Press; Rand, Avery, 1886), p. 21.
2. Bromley, p. 77.
3. *House Report No. 2044*, p. 10 (see chap. 4, note 25).
4. New York *Evening Post*, September 15, 1885.
5. *House Report No. 2044*, p. 10.
6. Isaac Bromley to Charles Adams, September 26, 1885, *UPR Records.*
7. St. Louis *Chronicle*, September 3, 1885.
8. Charles Adams to Samuel Callaway, September 26, 1885, *UPR Records.*
9. Adams to Calloway, September 8, 1885, *UPR Records.*
10. Adams to Calloway, September 26, 1885, *UPR Records.*
11. Callaway to Adams, September 9, 1885, *UPR Records.*
12. New York *Evening Post*, September 15, 1885.
13. *House Report No. 2044*, p. 30.
14. New York *Evening Post*, September 15, 1885.
15. Isaac Bromley to Charles Adams, September 21, 1885, *UPR Records.*
16. Adams to Callaway, October 19, 1885, *UPR Records.*
17. Adams to Callaway, date uncertain, *UPR Records.*

18. D. O. Clark to Callaway, September 16, 1885, *UPR Records*.
19. Bromley, p. 15.
20. D. O. Clark to Callaway, September 16,1885, *UPR Records*.
21. *House Report No. 2044*, p. 30.
22. Callaway to Adams, September 14, 1885, *UPR Records*.
23. Adams to Callaway, September 15, 1885,*UPR Records*.
24. Isaac Bromley to Adams, September 26, 1885,*UPR Records*.
25. Bromley to Adams, September 26, 1885, *UPR Records*.
26. Laramie *Daily Boomerang*, September 18, 1885.
27. D. O. Clark to Samuel Callaway, September 15, 1885, *UPR Records*.
28. Cheyenne *Sun*, September 10, 1885.
29. Samuel Callaway to Charles Adams, September 17, 1885, *UPR Records*.
30. Adams to Callaway, September 18, 1885, *UPR Records*.
31. Bromley, p. 21.
32. Bromley, p. 72.
33. Bromley, p. 73.
34. Charles Adams to Samuel Callaway, September 17, 1885, *UPR Records*.
35. Reported in Callaway to Adams, September 18, 1885,*UPR Records*.
36. Reported in Callaway to Adams, September 20, 1885, *UPR Records*.
37. Omaha *Herald*, o/a September 10, 1885, Warren Papers.
38. Bromley, p. 85.
39. Charles Adams to Samuel Callaway, September 21, 1885, *UPR Records*.
40. Adams to E. L. Godkin, September 18, 1885, *UPR Records*.
41. Bromley, p. 74.
42. D. O. Clark to Samuel Callaway, September 23, 1885, *UPR Records*.
43. Callaway to Charles Adams, September 23, 1885, *UPR Records*.
44. Callaway to Adams, September 25, 28, & 29,1885, *UPR Records*.
45. Callaway to Adams, October 3, 1885, *UPR Records*.
46. Adams to Callaway, October 1, 1885, *UPR Records*.
47. David G. Thomas, "David G. Thomas' Memories of the Chinese Riot," *Annals of Wyoming* 19, no. 2 (July 1947): 110.
48. *Daily Alta* (California), October 10, 1885.
49. Bromley, p. 78.
50. *The Nation*, October 13, 1885, p. 313.
51. Bromley, p. 80.
52. Bromley, p. 83.
53. John Mushet to Terence Powderly, October 12, 1885, Powderly Papers, Letter File: October–December 1885 (see note 19, chapter 5).
54. Terence Powderly to Thomas Neasham, October 31, 1885, Powderly Papers.
55. Bromley, pp. 89–90.
56. Samuel Callaway to Charles Adams, November 18, 1885, *UPR Records*.
57. Adams to Callaway, September 26, 1885, *UPR Records*.

CHAPTER EIGHT

Epigraph is from Arlen Ray Wilson, "The Rock Springs Wyoming Chinese Massacre, 1885" (master's thesis, University of Wyoming, 1967) p. 73.
1. Wilson, p. 73.
2. Francis Warren to General Schofield, September 27, 1885, F. E. Warren Papers, Letterbook 4-7-1890 to 11-15-1894, University of Wyoming Archives, Laramie, Wyo.
3. Isaac Bromley to Charles Adams, October 4, 1885, Warren Papers.
4. *Daily Alta* (California), September 13, 1885.

5.   Chung-Tsu Wu, *Chink!* (New York: World Publishing, 1972), p. 173.
6.   Chung-Tsu Wu, p. 173.
7.   Chung-Tsu Wu, p. 175.
8.   Chung-Tsu Wu, p. 176.
9.   Cheng Tsao Ju to Secretary of State Bayard, April 5, 1886, letter from the
     Chinese legation to the secretary, National Archives, Washington, D.C.
10. Chung-Tsu Wu, pp. 177–78.
11. Chung-Tsu Wu, p. 180.
12. Salt Lake *Daily Herald*, November 7, 1885.
13. Salt Lake *Daily Herald*, February 8, 1886.
14. Salt Lake *Daily Herald*, February 9, 1886.
15. Salt Lake *Daily Herald*, February 11, 1886.
16. *House Report No. 2044*, pp. 57–58 (see chap. 4, note 25).
17. *House Report No. 2044*, pp. 5, 56.
18. Mary Coolidge, *Chinese Immigration* (New York: Henry Holt, 1909), p. 183.
19. Salt Lake *Daily Herald*, February 23, 1886.
20. San Francisco *Examiner*, March 4, 1886.
21. *House Report No. 2044*, p. 2.
22. *House Report No. 2044*, p. 3.
23. *House Report No. 2044*, p. 2.
24. Coolidge, p. 183.
25. Isaac Bromley to Charles Adams, September 25, 1885, *Records of the Union
     Pacific Railway Company* (hereafter, *UPR Records*), (Lincoln: Nebraska State Hist.
     Soc.).
26. Charles Adams to Samuel Callaway, October 6, 1885, *UPR Records*.
27. Report of the Government Directors of the U.P. Railway Co., January 30, 1886,
     House Executive Documents, 49th Cong., lst sess., 1885–1886, vol. 12, p. 1235.
28. Cheyenne *Daily Leader* , September 16, 1885.
29. Isaac H. Bromley, *The Chinese Massacre at Rock Springs, Wyoming Territory*
     (Boston: Franklin Press; Rand, Avery, 1886), p. 93.
30. Adams to Callaway, October 5, 1885, *UPR Records*.
31. Adams to Callaway, October 6, 1885, *UPR Records*.
32. Laramie *Daily Boomerang*, October 24, 1885.
33. D. O. Clark to Isaac Bromley, December 20, 1885, *UPR Records*.
34. Adams to Callaway, January 30, 1886, *UPR Records*.
35. Norman Ware, *The Labor Movement in the United States* (New York: D.
     Appleton, 1970), p. 149.
36. Lt. Brennan to Adj. General Breck, February 9, 1887, Adjutant General's Office
     Files for 1885, National Archives, Washington, D.C.

BIBLIOGRAPHY

BOOKS

Ames, Charles Edgar. *Pioneering the Union Pacific.* New York: Century-Crofts, 1969.

Athearn, Robert. *High Country Empire.* New York: McGraw-Hill, 1960.

Barth, Gunther. *Bitter Strength.* Cambridge, Mass.: Harvard University Press, 1964.

Bartlett, I. S., ed. *History of Wyoming.* Chicago: S. J. Clarke, 1918.

Beard, Francis Birkhead. *Wyoming: From Territorial Days to the Present.* Chicago and New York: American Historial Society, 1933.

Beebe, Lucius, and Clegg, Charles. *The American West: The Pictorial Epic of a Continent.* New York: Bonanza Books, 1955.

Best, Gerald. *Iron Horses to Promontory* . San Marino, Calif.: Golden West Books, 1969.

Billington, Ray Allen. *Westward Expansion: A History of the American Frontier.* New York: Macmillan, 1974.

Bromley, Isaac H. *The Chinese Massacre at Rock Springs, Wyoming Territory.* Boston: Franklin Press, Rand, Avery, 1886.

Buchanan, Joseph. *The Story of a Labor Agitator.* Westport, Conn.: Greenwood Press, 1970.

Chen, Jack. *The Chinese of America.* San Francisco: Harper and Row, 1980.

Chung-Tsu, Wu. *Chink!* New York: World Publishing, 1972.

Clark, Marjorie, and Simon, S. Fanny. *The Labor Movement in America.* New York: W. W. Norton, 1938.

Coolidge, Mary. *Chinese Immigration.* New York: Henry Holt, 1909.

Davis, John P. *The Union Pacific Railway: A Study in Railway Politics, History and Economics.* New York: Arno Press, 1973.

Dietz, C. S. *The Developed and Undeveloped Mineral Resources of Wyoming.* Cheyenne: Wyoming Geological Survey, 1929.

Dodge, Grenville. *How We Built the Union Pacific Railway.* Washington, D.C.: Government Printing Office, 1910.

Erwin, Marie, ed. *Wyoming Historical Blue Book: A Legal and Political History of Wyoming 1868–1943.* Denver: Bradford-Robinson, 1947.

Gould, Lewis L. *Wyoming: A Political History.* New Haven, Conn.: Yale University Press, 1968.

Gowan, Fred, and Campbell, Eugene. *Ft. Bridger: Island in the Wilderness.* Provo, Utah: Brigham Young University Press, 1975.

Griswold, Wesley. *A Work of Giants.* New York: McGraw-Hill, 1962.

Grodinsky, Julius. *Jay Gould: His Business Career*. Philadelphia: University of Pennsylvania Press, 1957.

Groutage, Lorenzo. *Wyoming Mine Run*. Salt Lake City: Paragon Press, 1981.

Hebard, Grace Raymond. *Washakie*. Cleveland: Arthur H. Clark, 1930.

Hogg, Gary. *Union Pacific Railroad: The Building of the First Transcontinental*. New York: Walker, 1967.

Hollan, W. Eugene. *The Great American Desert, Then and Now*. New York: Oxford University Press, 1966.

Jones, Claire. *The Chinese in America*. Minneapolis: Lerner, 1972.

Kelly, Charles. *The Outlaw Trail*. New York: Devin-Adair, 1938.

Kraus, George. *High Road to Promontory*. Palo Alto, Calif.: American West, 1969.

Kung, S. W. *Chinese in American Life*. Seattle: University of Washington Press, 1962.

Larson, T. A. *History of Wyoming*. Lincoln: University of Nebraska Press, 1978.

Lewis, Oscar. *The Big Four*. New York: Alfred A. Knopf, 1938.

Linford, Velma. *Wyoming: Frontier State*. Denver: Old West, 1947.

McCague, James. *Moguls and Iron Men*. New York: Harper and Row, 1964.

McLeod, Alexander. *Pigtails and Gold Dust*. Caldwell, Idaho: Caxton, 1948.

Miller, Stuart. *The Unwelcome Immigrant*. Berkeley: University of California Press, 1969.

Nevins, Allan. *The Emergence of Modern America*. New York: Macmillan, 1927.

O'Connor, Richard. *Gould's Millions*. New York: Doubleday, 1962.

Orwell, George. *The Road to Wigan Pier*. Middlesex, U.K.: Penguin, 1984.

Pence, Mary Lou, and Homsher, Lola. *The Ghost Towns of Wyoming*. New York: Hastings House, 1956.

Rhode, Robert B. *Booms and Busts on Bitter Creek: A History of Rock Springs, Wyoming* . Boulder, Colo.: Pruett, 1987.

Sandmeyer, Elmer C. *The Anti-Chinese Movement in California*. Urbana-Champaign: University of Illinois Press, 1973.

Saxton, Alexander. *The Indispensable Enemy*. Berkeley: University of California Press, 1971.

Stansbury, Howard. *An Expedition to the Valley of the Great Salt Lake*. Ann Arbor, Mich.: University Microfilms, 1853.

Stewart, John. *The Iron Trail to the Golden Spike*. Salt Lake City: Deseret, 1969.

Sung, B. L. *The Story of the Chinese in America*. New York: Collier, 1971.

Trenholm, Virginia Cole, and Carley, Maurine. *The Shoshonis: Sentinels of the Rockies*. Norman: University of Oklahoma Press, 1964.

Tung, William L. *The Chinese in America*. Dobbs Ferry, N.Y.: Oceana, 1974.

Union Pacific Coal Company. *History of the Union Pacific Coal Mines 1868 to 1940*. Omaha, Nebr.: Colonial Press, 1940; reprint ed., Green River,

Wyo.: Sweetwater County Historical Society, 1977.
Union Pacific Passenger Department. *The Resources and Attractions of Wyoming.* St Louis: Woodward and Tiernan, 1891.
Wallace, Robert. *The Miners.* New York: Time-Life Books, 1976.
Ware, Norman. *The Labor Movement in the United States.* New York: D. Appleton, 1970.
Weiss, Melford. *Valley City: A Chinese Community in America.* Cambridge, Mass.: Schenkman, 1974.
Wollenburg, Charles, ed. *Ethnic Conflict in California History.* Los Angeles: Tinnon-Brown, 1970.
Wyoming Writers' Project. *Wyoming: A Guide to Its History, Highways, and People.* New York: Oxford University Press, 1941.

NEWSPAPERS

Brooklyn *Times*, September 5, 1885.
Cheyenne *Daily Leader*, June 18, 1873, November-December 1875.
Cheyenne *Democratic Leader*, September 17, 1885.
Cheyenne *Sun*, September 10, 1885.
Daily Alta (California), May 12, 1852, September 17, 1885, October 10, 1885.
Deseret News (Salt Lake), September 4, 1885.
Laramie *Daily Boomerang*, September 1885.
Laramie *Daily Sentinel,* November 1875.
Laramie *Daily Sun*, November 1875.
New York *Evening Post*, September 15, 1885.
New York Times, October 26, 1871, September 6, 1885.
Omaha *Herald*, September 10, 1885.
Pittsburgh *Telegraph*, September 5, 1885.
Rock Springs *Independent,* September 4, 1885.
Rock Springs *Miner*, September 30, 1950.
Rocky Mountain Daily News, September 14–15, 1885.
Sacramento *Record Union*, January 10, 1879.
St. Louis *Chronicle*, September 3, 1885.
Salt Lake *Daily Herald,* September 1885–March 1886.
Salt Lake *Daily Tribune,* September 1885.
San Francisco *Bulletin*, October 25, 1871.
San Francisco *Examiner*, March 4, 1886.

PERIODICALS

Annals of Wyoming, March 1940; July, November 1947.
The Nation, October 13, 1885.
Overland Monthly, October, November, December 1885.

Union Pacific Employees Magazine, March 1927.
Wyoming Labor Journal, August 31, 1917.

MANUSCRIPT COLLECTIONS

Adjutant General's Office Files for 1885. National Archives, Washington, D.C.
Powderly, Terence, Collection. Letter Files: 1885–1886. Catholic University, Washington, D.C.
The Union Pacific Railway Company, Records of. Nebraska State Historical Society, Lincoln, Nebraska. (Correspondence of Charles Adams, Samuel Callaway, S. H. H. Clark, and Sidney Dillon.)
Warren, Francis E. Papers. University of Wyoming, Laramie, Wyoming.

PUBLIC DOCUMENTS

U.S. Congress. House. Committee on Foreign Relations. *Report on Chinese Labor Troubles, House Report No. 2044.* 49th Cong., 1st sess., 1885–1886.
U.S. Congress. House. *Report of the Government Directors of the Union Pacific Railway Company, 1886.* H. Exec. Docs., 49th Cong., 1st sess., 1885–1886.
U.S. Congress. *Report of the Joint Committee to Investigate Chinese Immigration.* 45th Cong., 2d sess.
U.S. Congress. Senate. *Report of the Government Directors of the Union Pacific Railway Company, 1873.* S. Exec. Doc. 69, Serial 2336, 49th Cong., 1st sess. Government Printing Office, 1886.
U.S. Department of the Interior. *Special Report of the Governor of Wyoming to the Secretary of the Interior concerning Chinese Labor Troubles, 1885.* National Archives, Washington, D.C.

UNPUBLISHED MATERIALS

Fletcher, E. A. "History of the Labor Movement in Wyoming." Master's thesis, University of Wyoming, 1945.
Wilson, Arlen Ray. "The Rock Springs, Wyoming, Chinese Massacre, 1885." Master's thesis, University of Wyoming, 1967.

INDEX

Adams, Charles
  background, 105–6
  becomes president of Union Pacific,
    100
  opposes conciliation with Knights of
    Labor, 143, 144, 148
  and shopmen's strike, 100, 101
  urges government troops in Rock
    Springs, 131, 135, 137
  wants general strike, 144, 151, 153,
    154, 158
  worried about coal supply, 148
Ah Koon, 89, 111, 116
Ah Say
  asks U.S. government to keep troops
    in Rock Springs, 173, 174
  background, 89
  buys dragon, 91
  in Evanston, after massacre, 129, 136
  flees Chinatown, 116
Almy. *See* Evanston
Anti-Chinese movement
  anti-coolie clubs, 24
  congressional hearing, 29
  demonstrations against Chinese, 25
  and elections, 29
  incidents of violence, 28
  laws, 23, 24
  origins of, 21, 22
  reignited by Rock Springs massacre,
    159–69
  taxes, 23, 24
  and unemployment, 28
  Workingman's Party of California, 22

Bannock. *See* Shoshoni uprising
Bayard, Thomas A., 132, 137, 167
Bear Hunter, 38, 39
Beckwith, A. C.
  background, 73

policy toward white miners, 72, 83–85
threatened after massacre, 135, 137
Union Pacific contracts with, for
  Chinese, 66
Bitter Creek
  coal discovered at, 33
  description of, 49
  flooding, 50
Black Hills, 9, 11, 42, 43
Blair, Archibald and Duncan
  and building of stage station, 32
  can't compete with Union Pacific, 46,
    47, 55
  and opening of mine, 43
Buchanan, Joseph
  calls coal strike, 104, 105
  organizes coal miners, 102, 104
  and shopmen's strike, 101
  and Wabash strike, 143

Callaway, Samuel
  Charles Adams opinion of, 105
  and coal strikes, 104–7
  meets with grievance committee, 149,
    150
  reacts to news of massacre, 128
  tries to reopen Almy/Evanston, 149
Carbon
  coal strikes in 1885, 104–7
  first mine opened, 44
  mines seized by Union Pacific, 60
  production, compared with Rock
    Springs, 47
  strike after massacre, 154, 156, 157
  strike of 1875, 66, 67
Cassidy, Butch, 51, 52
Central Pacific Railroad, construction of
  Cape Horn, 12
  Chinese labor, use of, 10–15
  completion of, 19–21

189